# When Wisdom Speaks

## Living Experiences with Biblical Women

### Lyn Holley Doucet
### and Robin Hebert

*A Crossroad Book*
The Crossroad Publishing Company
New York

The Crossroad Publishing Company
16 Penn Plaza, 481 Eighth Avenue
New York, NY 10001

The text fonts are Sabon, Goudy Sans, and Benguiat.
The display font is Liberty.

Printed in the United States of America

**Library of Congress Cataloging-in-Publication Data**
Doucet, Lyn Holley, 1950-
    When wisdom speaks : living experiences with biblical women /
Lyn Holley Doucet & Robin Hebert.
        p.  cm.
    ISBN-13: 978-0-8245-2570-5 (alk. paper)
    ISBN-10: 0-8245-2570-1 (alk. paper)
    1. Women in the Bible.  I. Hebert, Robin.  II. Title.
BS575.D68 2007
0.9'2082 – dc22

                                                              2007002712

1   2   3   4   5   6   7   8   9   10        12   11   10   09   08   07

# When Wisdom Speaks

*To those on spiritual journeys*

Please know that we understand your ups and downs, the dark days and the bright moments — when unexpectedly you touch heaven. We know because we are walking the same rocky and grace-filled path that you are walking. This book is for you, our dear ones — to let you know that others so long ago walked along this same road. They traversed it with failure and with success, in many directions and in a hundred ways. Their trials and their victories belong to all of us; their stories help us to heal, help us to go on, help us to triumph.

# Contents

# A Word about the Book

An *epiphany* is described as "a feeling or a sudden realization or comprehension of the essence or meaning of something." So I had a minor epiphany about my role as an editor but not a full-blown epiphany about the meaning of life.

You would think after thirty years of working as an editor that I would have a fairly clear idea of what my role requires. Mostly, I think I do. But while working on this second book with Robin and Lyn, I learned something that I had not put into words before. It was that an editor's duties include first a request, and then encouragement, for writers to go deeper into their own souls and their own experiences so that they write from a place that they have never accessed before. It is a call to deep personal authenticity and it is also a call to a literary adventure. In other words, they will bare their own souls in a deeper way to readers, and they will write more honestly and elegantly than they have previously.

The experience of working on this book will always now remind me of those duties. Lyn and Robin certainly answered that call in their first book, *When Women Pray,* even though the duty to issue that call was not as clear to me then as it is now. And in this new book they have answered that call again.

In writing *When Women Pray* they entered into a spiritual journey that took them down deep within their own souls so they could write about their spiritual experiences in prayer. With this new book, *When Wisdom Speaks,* they have done that again, but they have also done something more. Imaginatively, and with that same sense of spiritual integrity, they have taken us into the lives and experiences of biblical women: Mary, Ruth, Sarah, Martha, Hannah, Mary of Magdala, and others. By doing this we learn valuable lessons about our own spiritual lives. Additionally, Lyn and Robin, along with these wise women whose lives shine through the biblical text, take us into a world wholly unlike our own — a Middle Eastern culture of long past. We are invited into that foreign world and find, unexpectedly, that it is for our own good. That is a major spiritual and literary accomplishment. Enjoy this journey, as it is a rare and fruitful one.

*Roy M. Carlisle*
*Editorial Consultant*

Women's stories need to be told and retold. For too long we have been deprived not only of a collective memory of women's accomplishments but also an understanding of the spiritual fiber they embodied in the struggles and challenges that are now ours. We need to hear their stories and remember our own; but even more we need their passionate faith so we can carry on our own work.

— Mary Ruth Broz, RSM, and Barbara Flynn,
*Midwives of an Unnamed Future*

Woman, with a candle lighted
To help her keep faith with her own life...
a centered presence
spreading in concentric circles around her.

— Judith Duerk, *Circle of Stones*

# Introduction

**RH** Last summer, just after Lyn and I had submitted the final revisions of our manuscript *When Women Pray*, I was already experiencing the void one feels after completing a creative accomplishment. Moreover, I was missing the connection that she and I had shared during our collaboration time, the blessed linking of our writing experiences and of our stories being lived out as the writing progressed. We had laughed and cried and prayed together over those sixteen months and had shared much more than a writing partnership. We had encountered each other's souls. I think that's what I was missing the most.

At that time, I was leading a book study group, using the text *A Woman after God's Own Heart,* with female college students and women from my church parish. As a spiritual director I always delight in the opportunity to offer a comforting environment where intimate sharing can occur and greater depth is achieved. Typical of my book study programs, I began each session by praying *Lectio Divina* with the group using a chosen passage from Scripture, so it made perfect sense to begin our classes connecting with women from the Bible — each a woman after God's own heart. I found myself looking forward every week to the choice of which woman's story we would share and with whom we would enter prayer. As we read the words surrounding their lives each session, I felt provoked by

11

the desperation of the Canaanite woman, empowered by Mary's fiat, affirmed by the loyalty of Mary Magdalene, and challenged by Ruth's fidelity (to a mother-in-law no less!) as well as by Hannah's relinquishment of her son.

Each prayed-with woman touched a different place on my own unfolding journey, and it was delightful to observe the same experience occurring in the other participants. All of the stories — the ancient ones, the accounts that were two thousand years old, and the current stories shared by the gathering women — remarkably linked all of our spirits together. By the end of the summer, I felt as if I had created a spiritual sisterhood not just with the beautiful souls that formed our community those eight weeks, but with those holy women who lived so very long ago and who ate and drank with Jesus — all of us women after God's very heart. I wanted more time with all of them and in fact continued the group into the fall. I found myself wanting to write about what was stirring in me, and I spoke one day with Lyn about the possibility of a new shared project.

We saw immediately how our differences would contribute to our writing as they had in *When Women Pray*. As a cradle Catholic, I grew up with a limited exposure to Scripture and came late to its appreciation. Under gifted spiritual direction, the Holy Spirit seemed to woo me into a craving for God's Word. I learned to trust my heart in prayer and discovered how famished my spirit had been without a daily connection to Scripture.

Although Lyn is an adult convert to the Catholic Church, her relationship with the Bible began in a Methodist Sunday school where Bible stories were told and retold. She knew that now, as those stories were retrieved, she would gain a more mature understanding of the lives they represented.

We recognized, too, that we grew up with very different role models of women of faith. Lyn's exposure to capable and strong, yet very feminine women in her church (who didn't ask permission to do things) was very different from my experience with nuns who were fierce disciplinarians and seemingly bowed to the priests' direction. They often didn't portray the soft feminine virtues that I craved in my own spiritual development, yet I found in my church the deep sense of awe and mystery that sustains me to this day. We had come at our shared faith from quite different places and knew it would be evident in our writing.

We noted, however, that our experiences as spiritual directors, as retreat leaders, and as Theresians immersed us in sharing, trusting, and growing alongside one another, and that our relationship could enable us to more deeply unite with the women we would be writing about. In addition, we agreed that we had come to trust our prayer experiences, that they would reveal, as they had in the past, a clarity and synthesis that could possibly open others to experience their own authentic walk.

We became excited about the possibilities of joining our creative energies once again.                         — R.H.

**LHD** On a crisp April morning, Robin and I sat on my sun porch and pondered the women of the Bible. We ate magic tuna sandwiches from Ray's Quickstop down the street in downtown Maurice. These sandwiches are famous; the recipe is simple, yet they feel like medicine for my body.

Robin and I munched and watched cardinals darting about the lawn, and rabbits making their brief appearances from behind the tallow trees before dashing away. We then centered ourselves in contemplation in order to discuss our call to write about the women of the Bible, and ponder how to create a new recipe for writing about them. We wondered whether we could stir the sacred alchemy between *us* as women and faith-friends and find the soul medicine that might again saturate our writing, bringing new energy and insight to this work, even though these women have been discussed at length by many other writers throughout the centuries.

I recalled my own Bible days growing up Methodist in a lovely old church in Bastrop, Louisiana. I was taught to read my Bible, but I wondered now: Did the women's stories just get lost among those of the men who seemed to be having all the adventures? Did I truly understand the importance of these women to Jesus's life and his ministry? And did the lack of awareness about these women exist in my own understanding and culture (southern girl of the fifties) or in those who taught me?

I could see myself in Sunday school coloring pictures of David and Goliath, Joshua who blew the walls down, and certainly Jesus. These male stories seemed filled with power. Then I learned that Eve lost God's grace and that Delilah took away Samson's power by cutting his hair. Oh dear, did I think then that Bible women had mostly to do with a *loss* of good things?

I remember generic pictures of some of these ancient women now — they wore cloths draped over their heads and carried olive jars — but I don't remember learning many of their names. And I clearly recalled the charming pictures of the holy family with Mary so tender and mild. However, looking back, my memories of holy *women* seemed as flat as the coloring book pages they handed out in Sunday school.

I didn't understand the importance of the New Testament women who had embraced Jesus's person and his mission. Yet the women who surrounded me in my church were clearly empowered and alive with faith. They loved me and accepted me, making me feel at home among them. Perhaps that was all I needed to bring me to this quest today.

As I grapple now with a new understanding of Bible women, I do so realizing that I'm all grown up (well, in many ways) and women's stories have become a passion for me. Today I ask how their stories and their very names got lost in the retelling, and I ask how we can uncover some of what was lost. These are basic questions: Who were they, and what really happened to them? And how does this affect all women and people of faith today?                                        —L.H.D.

## ~~ *Two Ways of Seeing* ~~ *These Women*

As our essays began to unfold, we saw two ways in which we could discover these women and embrace them. Both methods involved meditating and praying, holding the images of specific biblical women and their stories close to our hearts and minds as we did so. In the first way of relating we would actively seek to communicate with their spirits. In doing so, we would solicit "a word" or message for our spirits. We sought from these Bible sisters internal bits of wisdom and holiness that would enlarge us and keep us true to an authentic spiritual journey; we would be women with candles lighted, seeking to further understand our own lives.

We believed that these holy women would speak to us, because as Therese of Lisieux says, "I believe the blessed in heaven have a great compassion.... They remember that when they were frail and mortal like us they committed the same faults, endured the same struggles, and their love for us becomes greater even than it was on earth, this is why they do not stop ... praying for us."

In the other way of being with and writing about these women, we would prayerfully consider how their stories reported to us in the Bible are similar to our own. We would meditate about this, knowing that the way that God worked in *their* lives could inform us about the way God works in *our own* lives. For the stories of women are archetypal; recurring themes center around those things important and special to us — *as* women — and as women who long for God's heart. Ah, these dear women: battered, misunderstood, abused and challenged beyond hope — yet they found hope and holiness because God loved them. We sit before them now. We embrace them with love. Each one is truly our sister.

# SISTER

Sister,

You have rounded the corner just before me,

I see the scarlet of your sash disappearing from sight,

Now I hold in my hand a few linen threads from your
robe, caught on roughened parchment as you
hurried by.

They are golden with time, burned in an Eastern sun,

Speaking your story to me,

That once you embraced your husband under a canopy
of silk,

Nursed a baby as you walked a desert landscape in
search of water,

Sewed a tent, a bridal gown, a shroud.

Taught the secrets of Wisdom and remembered every
treasured story.

Sister,

I try to knit these wispy threads together, to piece a
fragment of your life for my life

From the scanty whispered words left behind,

The stencils faded and abandoned in a cave for long
winters,

Words written and not written,

Your name lost in the telling.

So how can I speak of your passions and skills, all the
ones who loved you?

And yet my sister, my grandmother,

you live within me now; your blood is in my very bones.

17

Sister,

Come to me,

Inhabit my dreams, and in my prayer, shadow me.

Tell me the secrets that ran from the page, tell me the
    truth of a woman

So much like me,

Beautiful, willful, gifted, hurt, triumphant.

Tell me the story of the Lord of Life,

Who came to you just as rosy sunset

Called forth the dancing fires within your hearth,

Yes, dancing warm and russet-red, their shadows large
    upon your walls.

Lighted by the One, Lover of Lovers,

Who drew you close and whispered soft your name.

—L.H.D.

# 1

# Mary and Elizabeth

## Blessed Am I Among Women

In those days Mary set out and went with haste to a Judean town in the hill country, where she entered the house of Zechariah and greeted Elizabeth. When Elizabeth heard Mary's greeting, the child leaped in her womb. And Elizabeth was filled with the Holy Spirit and exclaimed with a loud cry, "Blessed are you among women, and blessed is the fruit of your womb. And why has this happened to me, that the mother of my Lord comes to me? For as soon as I heard the sound of your greeting, the child in my womb leaped for joy. And blessed is she who believed that there would be a fulfillment of what was spoken to her by the Lord." —Luke 1:39–45

In everyone's life there is a great need for an anam ċara, a soul friend. In this love you are understood without mask or pretension. The superficial and functional lies and half truths fall away, you can be seen as you really are. Love allows understanding to dawn, and understanding is precious. When you are understood you are home. Understanding nourishes belonging. When you really feel understood, you feel free to release yourself into the trust and shelter of another's soul. —John O'Donohue, *Anam Ċara*

 I love the term *anam ċara*. The Gaelic words mean "soul friend." John O'Donohue poetically portrays this special type of companion, an "anam ċara," as a person to whom you can reveal the hidden intimacies of your life, a person of deep understanding, a shelter. When I imagine the visitation,

I envision a sacred encounter of two anam ċaras: Mary, searching for a sister, a soul to share her life-changing news, who found a safe haven where she could let down her guard and be loved deeply by another; and Elizabeth, who relished the supporting strength and companionship of her youthful cousin. The two women provided comfort for one another's souls, an offering of pure presence. I can't help but wonder whether the greatest anam ċara of all, Jesus, learned to be a soul friend in the presence of these women. Don't we all deserve such a sacred harbor?

God has indeed blessed my life with a legacy of anam ċaras, women who have taken me into their hearts and their homes during the more trying times in my life, sisters who cared for my soul and my deepest needs when I couldn't fathom taking care of my own. During a time of great uncertainty in my own life, two women in particular sheltered my heart and my family. Through their presence and care, my spirit sustained the transforming pains of labor that would eventually birth new life.

I had been visiting at my friend Barbara's home one ominous fall afternoon, only hours before my own annunciation. I had lain on her sofa nursing a stomachache, a confirmation my body offered that something just wasn't right. In my womb I must have known, as Mary had known, that soon my life would change irrevocably. Leaving Barbara's, I arrived home just in time to receive a phone call announcing the eventual demise of my marriage, a memory that even today carries a tiny pulse of pain. Barbara provided solace that day, and, over the years that followed, offered the comfort of her loving hospitality, sustaining me through the unfamiliar territory of dreaded change.

We fostered our friendship by establishing Mondays, my day off, as our special day for connecting. Thinking about those priceless visits helps me to imagine how Mary and Elizabeth might have spent their time together over the months they shared. Our visitation day became one of the touchstones in my life; we would walk in her neighborhood, chat in her living room, and sometimes cook together in her kitchen — often my zesty spaghetti sauce recipe. There were grim days when Barbara was challenged to bear my pain with me while I wept by her side. But mostly, there was a warm sense of presence and connectedness while my heart slowly mended and hers grew in compassion. In *When the Heart Waits,* Sue Monk Kidd speaks of our need to sit in one another's stillness and take up corporate postures of prayer, when we can be free enough to say to another, "I need you to wait with me," or "Would you like me to wait with you?" Barbara and I silently spoke such words to one another throughout those healing years.

As I'm sure must have been true for Mary and Elizabeth, our visits were often filled with joy. On some Mondays I arranged for my children to take the bus to Barbara's house after school, joining our two families. Our kids would all exit the bus gleefully, knowing that at least for an evening a visitation on a grand scale would take place along with a delicious meal shared at their large dining room table. To this day, the smell of simmering onions and roasting garlic offers a comforting remembrance of those precious times, even meals I shared with Barbara and her caring husband, Rick. Looking back on our friendship, I am filled with gratitude and the peace of knowing that each time Barbara and I gathered, I gained a bit more strength and a lot more grace for the continuing changes in my life.

My Theresian sister Ellen was another "Elizabeth" for me during those challenging times. She and I had found our way into our Open Heart Theresian community when our now twenty-three-year-old sons were infants. I love the warm sense of belonging that we all experience when our community meets in her home. I have discovered that walking into her kitchen is a stroll into Ellen's soul. Centered amid family memorabilia, her own beautiful paintings, treasured sentimental collections, and a large picture window offering a view of her lush, oak tree–studded backyard stands the setting for sacred meals, meetings, and gatherings — a large oval kitchen table, indeed an altar of grace. I have been among the countless privileged who have been nourished there, and I fondly remember the first time I dined at that table.

It was a dismal New Year's Day, my first as a single mom, the commencement of a new year that offered little hope and celebration for my family. As I gathered up the kids for Mass, I felt a much-needed sense of stability, even though I dreaded the loneliness I would bear without their dad at my side. My pain during Mass was fierce. Although the holidays were coming to an end, like a tidal wave, they had ravaged my heart and carried back to the sea my emotional belongings, leaving me with the barren reality that my sense of family would never be the same again. I sat in church trying to be strong for the kids and falling apart at the internal seams.

Turning toward the pew behind me during the sign of peace, I felt immediately warmed by Ellen's presence. I hadn't noticed that she and her lovely family were seated behind us, like a protecting shield. She could sense my pain. I could feel her compassion. I cried as we embraced, feeling like a stray with orphaned children. Without hesitation, Ellen affectionately whispered an invitation to join her family for dinner that day. I felt overwhelmed by her thoughtfulness, the kindness that has always surrounded Ellen. The kids and I spent a blessed day of belonging in her home, again linking together two families as one. My children and I were graced by a hospitable spirit that held us tenderly and offered hope in the midst of our turmoil. Like Mary, I had been offered a loving home, the heart of another woman. I felt the same comfort that she must have sensed in the arms of her cousin. Sister Joan Chittister speaks tenderly of this reality in *The Friendship of Women:* "Real friends are simply there for us, no matter the pressure, no matter the pain. They are home for us when no other home is open."* That is the soul of the Visitation.

The food offered at Ellen's and Barbara's tables was more than sustenance for the body. Like Mary, fearfully finding myself in unfamiliar territory, I was blessed with two Elizabeths who fed me in many ways and with countless others who held my hand and my heart during those tenuous years. The grace that God offered me was a consistent knowing that one of the best ways I could care for my soul was to claim time with my anam caras. Diverting the energy I might have spent on needless shopping and careless time-consuming activities, I nurtured the relationships my spirit most needed.

But we don't need loss and pain to cultivate soul friendships. All we need is the same hunger for intimacy and belonging that Mary and Elizabeth shared. At the heart of the Visitation rests a desire for deep sustaining friendships that we women

---

*Joan Chittister, *The Friendship of Women: A Spiritual Tradition* (Erie, Pa.: Benetvision, 2000).

must nourish because we need them as much as we need to come up for air in the ocean of our stress-filled lives. My friendship with Ellen has sustained me for a quarter of a century. Her kitchen table, where I'd sat on that painful winter day, was a setting of celebration ten years later. Ellen, our friend Carolyn, and I gathered for lunch just days before my marriage to Easton, lightheartedly calling our sacred meal my bridesmaid's luncheon.

One of the greatest sustaining sources of anam ċaras in my life has been my Theresian community. For over twenty-three years, my Open Heart sisters have gathered for a monthly visitation, lasting from morning coffee through shared lunch with lots of time for building intimacy and strengthening faith in between. I find our meetings reminiscent of that historical gathering of holy women in Luke's Gospel, as we seventeen Theresians have stood with each other, offering a holy presence to one another in the best and worst of times. We shared hospital duty when our sister Georgia's cancer threatened her life and held each other close in the church pew at her funeral. My sisters cried with me during the turmoil of my divorce and rejoiced at the announcement of my second marriage ten years later. We have prayed together, called forth each other's gifts, gathered our husbands, challenged growth in one another, and are now beginning to collectively age, gracefully I believe. Mostly we have come to see each other as God sees us. On the fourth Thursday of every month, we gather as women of shared faith, taking up "corporate postures of prayer," bringing to each other the presence of God. We are indeed each other's soul friends.

These and so many other women have in their healing embrace taught me to be an anam ċara. Of course my ministry as a spiritual director offers that safe presence for a longing soul, but sometimes just a hug, a phone call, a card, or a compliment can present a needed touchstone, an inkling of hope, a harbor from the storm. I have come to recognize that the gift that is given is always returned, for by its very nature, a visitation is a mutual affair. Elizabeth's warm hospitality and caring heart were reciprocated by Mary's service of assisting her hostess through the last trimester of her pregnancy. They gave life to one another. I never reach out to another without my own heart being touched.

If we look closely at our own lives, we will notice a myriad of visitations, times when we are blessed with opportunities to both give and receive love. My friend Pat shared with me recently about a visit to her nephew's home to assist his lovely wife and brand-new baby while her nephew was attending a family reunion with the older children. Pat spoke of her chance to be alone with that precious infant, embracing the wonder of innocence and pure love that was surely its gift back to her. Pat's offering of reassurance and attendance to the new mother was returned with love at a time when Pat felt inadequate and hopeless. The gift given is always returned.

What is it about women friendships that are such a gift and enable us to give birth to new things? What do women have to offer one another that is different from anything else in our lives? Looking once more to our sacred sisters in Scripture for guidance in cultivating the art of visitation, I see an inherent mutual understanding of one another. Lyn and I celebrate a visitation every time we gather to read our new essays or reveal our latest dreams. While writing has been the thread, discussing our everyday concerns has been the fabric of our growing friendship. We comprehend each other's mood swings and changing self-esteem barometers. We understand hormone patches and ailing husbands. In the grace of the present moment, we have eased our anxious hearts, grasped a deep appreciation of one another's needs, celebrated the new life of two books, and experienced the freedom to sing and proclaim the glory of God in our lives, as did Mary. We have often lifted one another's spirits with the sacred reminder, "Blessed is she who believed."

While Mary and Elizabeth's historical visitation supposedly lasted for three months, sometimes our modern-day visitations last the length of a phone call or the duration of a hospital visit. In its purest essence, a visitation is a communion, a Eucharist. Perhaps even prayer in its finest expression is a blessed visitation between two anam ċaras, where in the sacred space of love, understanding and belonging are divinely fused.

If we women are to give substance to our lives, we need lots and lots of visitations, quality time with soul friends when we can edge past our masks and breathe life into one another's souls. Stasi Eldredge underscores our heart's vast capacity for meaningful relationships in her wonderful book *Captivating:* "There is no way your husband or your children can ever provide the intimacy and relational satisfaction you need. A woman *must* have woman friends. To have a woman friend is to relax into another soul and be welcomed in all that you are and all that you are not."* God has blessed me from birth with anam ċaras. My soul proclaims the greatness of the Lord.

---

*John and Stasi Eldredge, *Captivating: Unveiling the Mystery of a Woman's Soul* (Nashville: Thomas Nelson, 2005).

MARY AND ELIZABETH, you have shown all women our need for one another, prompting us to let down our masks, rid ourselves of pretense, and let the arms of love enfold us in a transforming embrace. Thank you both for helping us to see that no matter what the circumstances of our lives might be, they are best shared in the sacred space of another woman, where tender care and understanding can divide our pain and multiply our joy. Blessed are we all among women.     —R.H.

### ELIZABETH

Elizabeth, my heart bounds high to see you,
You recognize me, crinkling with a smile.
I am not Mary, sinless one, but ah—a woman,
Filled with hidden darkness, secret light.

Our meeting is a sacred ground of waiting
And secrets shared and joy that dares cry out.
But now we hold each other barely breathing,
For in each one there beats a newer life.

I hear you say, be blessed, for you are mother and
I wonder, could I know what that might mean? See
Crystal stars, hear whispered songs of shepherds
And angels hovering close upon the earth?

Then eyes are startled, mine so brown, yours lighter,
Startled by the force of so much light,
You wonder why few see the depth of blessing,
That calls us forth to Bethlehem's dark night.

Where Love from Love was given to a girl child,
The one you held so closely to your breast,
And songs burst from the hills and gold was gently laid,
And every child received from Love a gift.

I wonder if my heart can stay within me,
I ask if I will have my cherished hope—and all my dreams.
You ask me to release myself from knowing,
To find what you hold deep within yourself.

You laugh; you stroke my hair, and whisper comfort,
For things are never as they seem, you say.
To dance with Mystery is to be woman,
To love the thing unseen, our song, our life.

—L.H.D.

## A Special Community of Women

Theresians is a contemporary Catholic/Christian organization for women that provides a global network of small faith communities. Theresians was founded in 1961 in Pueblo, Colorado, by Monsignor Elwood Voss, who felt that there was little contemporary inspiration for women in the Catholic Church. Voss saw that "women were accustomed to giving of themselves in church and society, but were not often provided with in-depth opportunities for self-enrichment and spiritual growth. His solution was an organization that would provide women with an opportunity to enrich their own lives through spiritual development, ongoing education, affirmation and encouragement in their vocations, a deep community experience, and a ministry to others.*

Theresians are committed to a *way of life* that integrates five dimensions: spirituality, education, vocation, community, and ministry. Within small faith communities, from twelve to twenty women in each group, Theresians pledge support by prayerfully nurturing, affirming, and empowering each other to become the woman God intends her to be. Groups meet monthly in one another's homes to study, pray, and break bread together. But far from being serious study sessions, these meetings are experiences of joyful and sharing community.

For further information about Theresians, visit their Web site at *www.Theresians.org.*

---

*See Elwood C. Voss, Patricia Mullen, et al., *The Theresian Story: Women in Support of Women,* 2nd ed. (Washington, DC: Theresian Publications, 1996), 1–2.

**2**

# Martha

## I Discovered the One Thing

But the Lord answered her, "Martha, Martha, you are anxious and troubled about many things; one thing is needful. Mary has chosen the good portion, which shall not be taken away from her."

—Luke 10:41

Martha showed her devotion by giving the gift she knew best. The gift of service — but even welcome wagons can grow heavy, as Martha quickly discovered. Especially when they're laden with the extra weight of our human agendas and expectations.

—Joanna Weaver, *Having a Mary Heart in a Martha World*

"Now, don't discount Martha, my sisters. Don't forget that she is *Saint* Martha."  —Father Hampton Davis, talk to Theresian National Conference, October 2006

**LHD** Despite growing consciousness about the changing roles of women in our society, women still generally expend the most energy caring for the home, cooking the meals, and acting as the social glue that holds family and community together. As women, we have loved our roles of service and hated them.

And so, we consider the one who wrestled with the same issues so long ago. Yes, her — Martha-Martha.

As I close my eyes, I can see her; and in the middle of her forehead is a wrinkled line of worry. (I can hardly imagine the work she must have put forth when a recipe for bread began with "thresh the wheat.") It seems that she was expected to cook and serve the meal for Jesus and probably his twelve disciples and others. Then, when she asked for help, she was given a puzzling answer. I see her frustration as she watched her younger sister relaxing at Jesus's feet, free from the grind that was consuming Martha. It's all very well to say, "One does not live by bread alone," when the bread is mixed, kneaded, and baked by another.

What could Jesus have been trying to say to Martha that day in her home? Could he have been talking about choice? What choices did Martha have? Far fewer in her day and time than we have today, though we still struggle to meet the expectations of those around us, just as Martha did. Ah, my dear sisters, I believe that often we are trying to be perfect. And in being perfect we hope to earn our heart's desire — we hope to earn love.

My mind drifts back to a Christmas twenty years ago when I was hosting my entire extended family for several days. My cleaning and sorting began in November and went on relentlessly for days. My husband wanted to duck when he saw me coming with yet another list of things for him to do, but I was far harder on myself. I looked at those beautiful magazine spreads with the perfect meals and the happy families, and I was determined to re-create them. My Christmas celebration needed to be not just good, but absolutely wonderful. I never asked myself why. I never let myself acknowledge the worried little girl inside of me who tried too hard. I just pressed on, harder and harder. My Christmas became not about sharing love but about creating theater. I was to be the star of a beautiful play, and everyone was to be amazed and burst into applause.

The day finally came when the ten guests arrived. Every surface was gleaming and decorated to perfection. However, thirty minutes after my family arrived, the sink in the kitchen stopped working. My dad had to gather some tools and go under the cabinet to find the problem. To help him, my sister removed a large bag of dog food that had been stored under the sink. It turned out that (unbeknownst to me) the sink had been leaking and had soaked the bag. As my sister, Minnett, moved it, the bag broke, pouring dog food all over the spotless kitchen floor.

There we stood: no water, a sweating father, an apologetic sister, and a wrecked kitchen. I don't remember whether I cried. Looking back on this (now) amusing scene, it seems like poetic justice. Could Spirit have tried any harder to say, "Ah, Lyn, Lyn. Look at this. After you have worried about so many things. You forgot that only one thing was necessary. You could have saved yourself so much grief."

"One thing?" I might have replied. "Not a million things, but one thing? What does that mean?"

Twenty years after the spilled dog food Christmas, sitting here at my keyboard, I stop typing and close my eyes. Yes, there she is just behind my closed eyelids: Martha, with the crease in her forehead and the ache in her heart. I believe that she had a frightened child within her too, or perhaps a frightened woman. We aren't told what her growing up with Lazarus and Mary had been like. We don't know how she came to internalize the message that she must not only provide sustenance but do it perfectly. I wonder when she got cut off from who she really was and from her own feelings? I only know that Jesus found Martha in a dark place, angry and bitter in her struggle to earn love. She was acting out a role that concerned itself less with the happiness of others and more with perfect performance of her task. Perhaps Mary had spent the morning working with Martha, and now wanted to give Jesus her full attention. Maybe Martha was continuing to do things that had already been done, because she felt that nothing was ever good enough and she couldn't relax.

And perhaps Martha was a person who could not ask for help with *vulnerability*, having to demand it with anger and righteousness. I think she was a person who had never received the love she needed to blossom into a complete person. She was stuck in her roles, her martyrdom, unable to freely give love to others. Yet I also believe that Martha had a good heart. She was doing the best she could, and I feel a deep affection for her and kinship with her. She was about to learn more about love and be freed, perhaps, from some of her compulsions.

Love. That *is* the one thing necessary, isn't it? Isn't it love that can rescue us from living a lie that life is all about performance? Isn't it love that lets us admit when we're tired and we really don't want to do one more thing? Isn't it love that allows us to stop making unreasonable demands upon ourselves? And isn't it love, and its sister, humility, that can release us from chains that may be of our own making? Is this what Mary understood?

In my fondest imaginings now, I see both Mary and Jesus himself entering the kitchen where Martha was slaving away. I see them giving Martha a hug and a kiss as they thank her for all the work that she has done. I see Jesus hoist the big pot with the lamb roast on his shoulder, taking it to the table. Then I see him pulling out a chair for Martha. Perhaps he would say, "Welcome to the banquet, Martha, that has been set for you. Now you must do nothing else but be here with us. This is all we need, your presence. Be at peace, for we love you. We love you." (And I hope that Jesus and Mary washed all the dishes!)

I WANT TO INVITE JESUS to enter my own home and be with me in all its rooms. I know that he is willing to come into my kitchen and lift me up when compulsion and fear threaten to override my hospitality to others. Jesus feeds me from his very own hand when I remember that love is the one thing necessary, that all else is a fabrication to feed my ego. When I deal with my fear of others disapproving of me or finding me lacking, Jesus calls sweetly, "Don't forget; only one thing is necessary."

While I don't always listen well, I want to. I don't want to miss the banquet that Jesus himself sets, a table more beautiful than any magazine photograph could ever be. His is the banquet I long for, his the table of freedom, peace, and love.

—L.H.D.

3

# Martha

## *I Want the Better Part*

Now as they went on their way, he entered a certain village, where a woman named Martha welcomed him into her home. She had a sister named Mary, who sat at the Lord's feet and listened to what he was saying. But Martha was distracted by her many tasks; so she came to him and asked, "Lord, do you not care that my sister has left me to do all the work by myself? Tell her then to help me." But the Lord answered her, "Martha, Martha, you are worried and distracted by many things; there is need of only one thing. Mary has chosen the better part, which will not be taken away from her."

—Luke 10:38–42

Six days before the Passover Jesus came to Bethany, the home of Lazarus, whom he had raised from the dead. There they gave a dinner for him. Martha served, and Lazarus was one of those at the table with him.                         —John 12:1–2

The problem with the Martha-state is not with actions themselves, of course. Most of the saints lead extremely active lives. The difference lies in what is at the center of one's life. The human condition tempts me to put my actions at the center of my life. In the Martha-state, I work for God, but it is still *my* work that is at the center of my life. Everything is different for the saint. For her, actions are the offspring of God's lordship in her life. They are God's actions being done through her.         —Father Mark Thibodeaux, *Armchair Mystic*

 Of all the explanations I have ever read of the story of Mary and Martha, the famous sisters with the extremely different temperaments, I like Father Mark Thibodeaux's the best, found in his helpful prayer resource, *Armchair Mystic*, and quoted above in the epigraph. He seems to wisely artic- ulate the core message in Luke's Gospel: make surrendering to God your life project. Father Richard Rohr underscores the issue of marrying prayer with service when he explains creatively in *Everything Belongs* that the most important word in the title of his "Center for Action and Contemplation" is not "action" nor even "contemplation," but *and*. Father Rohr's comments speak to me of my desire to have my life reflect both prayer and action — actions that are anchored in God's will and not my own.

I learned a valuable lesson last summer, discovering as Martha did that if my work doesn't come from a surrendered heart, then it's not mine to do in the first place. My discovery happened during hurricane season when all of us living in southwest Loui- siana were in some way affected by the catastrophic winds and waters of change. While countless residents were directly dis- tressed by hurricanes Katrina and Rita and most of us had family and friends that faced property and emotional loss, all of us were supremely disturbed by the gruesome reality of Mother Nature's fury. Eeriest of all was how Lafayette stood spared (for the most part) as cities just east, west, and south of us were ravaged. I now understand survivor's guilt, the burdensome sense of re- sponsibility that emerges when one is standing unscathed in the midst of another's loss.

When the dust of the first storm, Katrina, had settled and the floodwaters were subsiding, our local shelters began filling up, sending most folks in Lafayette scrambling to help out. My own restlessness was a call to get to work. I would be surprised by what that work would look like.

My first inclination was to offer my counseling skills at the Cajundome, a central shelter that would house thousands of refugees. But the fitting time for me to get over there simply didn't present itself. The semester at the university where I work in ministry had just begun, filling up our campus with refugee students from closed universities along with our own struggling students who were feeling the stress of tenuous times. Moreover, my husband, Easton, was still recovering from a July back surgery and even then in September needed my help at home. Still, guilt and anguish were churning inside, and I could hear my own warning proclamation, "Robin, Robin, you are anxious and worried about many things" — the call to prayer.

Honestly, I hadn't thought to ask God what he wanted from me. My urge to offer help to anyone had always seemed accompanied by God's seal of approval, but I've come to see, as Martha did, that action without prayer is often my own work at the center of my life, my own need to feel needed, and in this case my own desire to feel important. What I heard in prayer that morning were these distinct words: "Thank you for all you are doing. It is enough." I smiled inside and breathed a sigh of relief, even though — at least temporarily — I had to surrender my curiosity about all the happenings at the Cajundome through the stories I'd been hearing from volunteers, including my own adult children. What God seemed to be telling me on that Tuesday morning, my day off, was to stay home and tidy the house, cook, and tend to Easton. It was truly freeing to obey the voice of wisdom.

An amazing thing happened that very afternoon. My daughter Megan, who had been volunteering at the Cajundome by helping out one particular family with errands and supplies,

called to see if I could help *her* out. She'd taken Sombi, a pregnant mother, to the hospital for tests and requested a helping
hand with Sombi's four-year-old daughter, who was in need
of lunch at three o'clock that afternoon. When Megan's white
minivan pulled up in my driveway, I dashed outside to greet
them. Out of the car jumped a tiny little girl who lunged into
my arms. Megan followed, walking up to introduce us: "Mom,
meet Robin." Joy swept my heart as I hugged the child bearing
my name, feeling her little arms tight around my neck. We embraced each other like we were old friends. Little Robin and I
shared a wonderful afternoon — a peanut butter and jelly sandwich and a lovely story book. The Cajundome had come to me.
I did what I was told and still got to do what I had wanted to
do in the first place. I wonder whether Martha praying before
that famous meal could have eased her anxious heart and provided clarity about what she was supposed to do. Perhaps her
serving would have been more joyous. (Truly it had only been
her worry and anxiety with which Jesus had taken offense, not
her actions.)

I did make it to the Cajundome, a few weeks later, after Hurricane Rita anchored our already despairing hearts in a mire of
hopelessness. I was sitting in a session with one of my directees, a young blind woman with a heart of gold, when she
tearfully expressed her frustrations of not having a ride to the
Cajundome where she wanted to volunteer. The voice inside me
was clear and emphatic: "Get her there." The following Friday
we spent a glorious afternoon feeling as though we were sitting
at the feet of Jesus — actually about six evacuees with few belongings, sitting on army cots in makeshift living rooms, telling
their tales of terrifying survival and uncertain futures.

A friend recently exposed a new element in Martha's saga, an inspiring interpretation of Martha's reappearance in the Gospel of John. I had only been acquainted with Luke's infamous exploration of Martha's struggle with worry and anxiety. As it turns out, Martha had serving roles in two different Gospels. Regarding the unfamiliar version, my friend offered the fresh insight that Martha's heart had been transformed since Jesus's loving reproach. Martha now seemed accepting of her role, at ease with her choice to serve. Maybe Martha was now more at ease with herself. In my imaginings, Martha had experienced a conversion of heart and had taken Jesus's advice seriously, perhaps even sat at his feet on occasion in a posture of listening. However it had happened, Martha's heart now seemed undivided. My friend explained, "When our heart is integrated, pure, and seamless, we can be involved in many things, because there isn't a tension." Recognizing that anxiety and tension are manufactured when my actions are at the center of my life will probably be an ongoing discovery for me.

At a time in my life when I was fiercely struggling with my "inner Martha," I heard an especially helpful explanation of one of the ways that God communicates with us. The words of wisdom came to me in spiritual direction with Father Hampton Davis. I had plopped down in a chair in his office, let out a loud sigh, and then bravely admitted my busyness to Father with this proclamation: "I'm running on my hamster wheel again!"

His response was quick: "What are you running from?"

"God, I guess," I said, thinking out loud about my resistance to slowing down.

"What are you afraid of?" he questioned.

"I'm afraid that if I stop long enough, I might hear God asking me to do something I don't want to do!"

His response was amazingly helpful: "Robin, God won't send you to Africa unless he first puts Africa in your heart." Father Hampton understood this wisdom, first spoken by Father Michael Scanlon, to be true (as I do now) — that we will want to do the work God calls us to. Our hearts will naturally draw us toward right action if we but listen to them. However, God won't be able to put anything in our lives if we do not take the time to listen in prayer, which was Father Hampton's point that day. I suppose that's what Martha learned in her time with Jesus. Perhaps she began to listen to her heart, where her opportunities for service were revealed through the love and peace that God had placed there.

I continue to ponder these all-important questions: How do I immerse myself in the busy world and at the same time keep my heart open before the Lord? How can I maintain a pure, seamless, and integrated heart? How do I honestly determine what is mine to do and what is mine not to do? I will certainly never do it perfectly, but I am gradually learning to turn my focus inward first, looking for the good spirit of strength and encouragement, consolation and inspiration, knowing that God's call for action is placed deep within my heart. In his interpretation of the Spiritual Exercises, *Draw Me into Your Friendship*, David Fleming, S.J., offers sound advice on discerning any course of action: "If in reflecting on the course of our thoughts and our actions we find that from beginning to end our eyes have remained fixed on the Lord, we can be sure that the good spirit has been moving in us."* Keeping my eye and heart fixed on the Lord is indeed my aim, although I know at times I will surely fail.

In the end, Martha's service to Jesus in the Gospel of John seemed authentic and true, the most honorable way she could show her love to her beloved Friend. I imagine that he must have appreciated her actions just as much as those of her adoring sister, whose love was literally poured out all over Jesus, sacramentally offered through the most precious thing she possessed, a bottle of expensive perfume. But Martha's kitchen skills were the most prized offering she had to present to him. And thank God we are all so different with our varying gifts and talents.

I am coming to understand that all our deeds, when offered through pure, filled hearts, add a sacred dimension to our world, each like a thread when woven together forms a beautiful tapestry. I must believe that sharing an insignificant PB&J sandwich and using my skills to listen with love to another person's story of trauma impacted Jesus as much as either of those two women's actions of love, all so very different yet unique to each of our precious souls and distinctive calls. Martha's important role in the Gospels finally makes sense to me. So does my own.

MARTHA, THANK YOU for modeling a heart of service, for reminding me that I can't just sit at the feet of Jesus — I must get up and do something. Might I always remember that I need to first seek Jesus's love to animate my own heart, and that the only thing I ever need to do is to follow his spirit willingly where it leads.                                                  — R.H.

---

*David Fleming, S.J., *Draw Me into Your Friendship: The Spiritual Exercises, A Literal Translation and a Contemporary Reading* (St. Louis: Institute of Jesuit Sources, 1996), 263.

# 4

# *Mary of Bethany*

## *How Could You Love a Woman Like Me?*

"One thing is needful. Mary has chosen the good portion, which shall not be taken away from her." —Luke 10:42

He mine by gift, I his by debt, thus each to other due. First friend he was, best friend he is, all times will Try him true.
— Saint Robert Southwell, S.J., *Hearts on Fire*

It is important to think about the Church not as "over there," but as a community of struggling, weak people of whom we are a part and in whom we meet our Lord and Savior.
— Henri Nouwen, *Bread for the Journey*

 I relate deeply to Mary of Bethany because I think we are similar in personality. Few in my life have said of me, "Let's give that job to Lyn because she is the practical one." Creative one, smart one, funny one, contemplative one — perhaps. *Not* the practical one.

We are all born, I think, with certain hardwired personality characteristics. And along with my personality (my basic way of being in this world) comes the approval of some people and the puzzlement of others. I wonder how Mary of Bethany coped with the opinions of others and how she had the courage to sit at the feet of Jesus. A woman of her day, time, and station did not receive teaching from a rabbi. Her sister, practical sister,

Martha, exemplifies this disapproval by asking Jesus to send Mary, in effect, back to the kitchen where she belonged. But Mary was secure sitting at the Master's feet and concerning herself with things of the Spirit. What can we learn from her?

I go to my prayer space and close my eyes, trying to see this woman, asking her to teach me. I communicate with her in spirit and seek to know her better.

*Mary, the Scriptures tell us that you were not the practical one; your sister Martha took that role. Were you a dreamy girl? Were you, like me, labeled "too sensitive"? Did you lose things and forget things, Mary? You were probably not the neat one. Perhaps you didn't have a sense of direction (like me) and got lost going to the butcher shop. I am sure you drove Martha to distraction many times. As I wonder what you were like, I know that you were shaped by a myriad of things that helped to fashion your relationship with your faith.*

*Why is this important to me, Mary of Bethany? It is because if there is one thing that every heart longs for — in its deepest and most vulnerable space — it is unconditional acceptance and love. This is what Jesus gave to you. He understood that you were different from your practical sister, and he embraced you. Were you quirky, questing, idealistic? You were certainly intuitive, as I am, and you were contemplative, lost in thought while others did the outer work. And Jesus accepted you and praised you for your very differences. Therefore, I feel I can rest in Jesus's unconditional acceptance of me too. I am loved because of, not in spite of, the way I don't always fit into the world, just as you were accepted and praised by him. In fact, because of you, Mary, I dare to think that I have chosen the better way.*

In my mind's eye, I see Mary of Bethany as a beautiful and feminine woman, one who expresses welcoming and soulful attention in her eyes and in her posture. I see in her also a symbol of the intuitive feminine, not naïve as I might have once thought she was, but wise and aware of the deep stirring of Spirit, a Spirit that moves where it will. In my imagination Mary smiles at me, acknowledging me as a sister in prayer.

Mary came again to me, in an unexpected way. I was outside on a brilliant blue-skied Sunday when the air was cool and the sun was warm. I was taking a walk along my accustomed route, deeply discouraged. Recent events had caused me to wonder if women would ever assume greater leadership roles in our church. Although I had no personal desires to do this, I longed for women as a whole to expand their roles in new ways.

My pain had increased when I tried to express my frustrations to others and had received varied responses from disappointed (in my attitude) to indifferent, discounting, and smug, with only an occasional person understanding the desires of my heart.

I wanted to understand why change came so slowly in the church and not feel resentful or alienated from my faith. Could I take Henri Nouwen's words to heart and realize that human organizations never meet the expectations of all their members? Could I, as he states further in his text, "forgive the church — as a fallible, human organization"? This seemed to be the right, measured response.

I thought about my Methodist roots and the dynamic Methodist women who were pastors, one in particular with whom I had worked. But I didn't feel called to return to that faith tradition. I was weary of my mood swings surrounding this issue: upset one minute only to numb myself and pretend I didn't care the next.

I puzzled about myself sometimes: why did I care about so many things that didn't seem to concern others? As I walked across the amber grass on that bright day, I thought about Mary of Bethany, a woman with few rights and a limited role, a woman who would have been discounted completely by the religious leaders of her day. As I stopped to rest, surrounded by bright yellow flowers and warmed by a vibrant, splashing sun, I asked the spirit of Mary to come down and stand with me. I asked her to inform my hurting heart and mind.

As I prayed with her, I heard these words, "Go to the Source; that's what I did."

"Go to the Source," I thought. "Try to leave behind the periphery of faith, at least for a time. Try to remember Jesus, who ministered to Mary of Bethany in a world where feminine wisdom and presence were held in low esteem. Mary of Bethany sat at the feet of the Source of life. She was intimate with the one who in some mysterious way *made her as she was* and loved her for *all* that she was: woman, disciple, mystic, misfit, contemplative, odd one, again, *woman.* Together in their sacred encounters they went to the heart of what really mattered: God's unconditional love and acceptance of each and every person equally, and Jesus's invitation to all, especially the little and overlooked ones, to come without fear to the table of Love."

After Mary of Bethany guided me to the Source that day, my heart was comforted by Love. Returning home after my walk, I took a shovel and dug deep into the dark, moist earth to plant jonquil bulbs. The dry, brown bulbs seemed to have no life within them. But I had faith that in the spring they would bloom, bringing new life in their creamy, feminine blossoms and the delicate green of their leaves. Planting bulbs is an act of hope, and hope was what I needed on that day. I felt fortified for my journey; hope had been renewed deep within me, where it kept company with my passion and my love.

MARY, I LOVE your passion; you showed it freely. You loved Jesus with an eros love that while not sexual, was particular. You loved him completely for the person he was, different from all other men. And he loved you too, deeply, warmly. In acknowledgment of this mutual love, you made the lavish gesture of smashing the perfume vessel and filling the house with the fragrance of all that was between you — understanding, affection, acceptance, honor, and grief. You, Mary, the passionate one and the intuitive one, you alone embraced Jesus's impending death.

How did you survive Jesus's death, Mary of Bethany? Ah, you tell me that you were present at the raising of Lazarus. That you knew you would see Jesus again. Therefore your deep and passionate grief hurt you for many years, but did not overwhelm you.

I have much of your passion, Mary, and your contemplative stance — I pray for your deep and womanly faith. Jesus embraced all of this in you; I hope that he sees it in me as well.

Faith is never an easy road. And so I pray that Jesus's unconditional love continues to feed me, giving me the courage to
embrace and love the person I was created to be as I walk the
path he calls me to, however gray or tense it may sometimes
be. At this moment, I think that I can walk my path in peace
and love as you did, intimately close to the heart of the Lord.

—L.H.D.

# 5

# The Canaanite Woman

## Lord, Help Me

Just then a Canaanite woman from that region came out and started shouting, "Have mercy on me, Lord, Son of David; my daughter is tormented by a demon." But he did not answer her at all. And his disciples came and urged him, saying, "Send her away, for she keeps shouting after us." He answered, "I was sent only to the lost sheep of the house of Israel." But she came and knelt before him, saying, "Lord, help me." He answered, "It is not fair to take the children's food and throw it to the dogs." She said, "Yes, Lord, yet even the dogs eat the crumbs that fall from their masters' table." Then Jesus answered her, "Woman, great is your faith! Let it be done for you as you wish." And her daughter was healed instantly.

— Matthew 15:22–28

Has it ever occurred to you that Jesus might be impressed with your faith, your hope, your love? Has it ever occurred to you that because of your single, pure, undivided heart, Jesus might look at you with love and say, "I like what I see. Your faith nourishes me. I can do nothing but respond to your great need. Be it done for you as you desire"? — Macrina Wiederkehr, *A Tree Full of Angels*

Try to acquire the virtues which you believe lacking in your brothers. Then you will no longer see their defects, because you will no longer have them yourselves. — Saint Augustine, Commentary on Psalm 30

 I cannot read the story of the Canaanite woman without sadly embracing the vulnerability of every mother. The reality is this: daughters have demons. And the demons range from mild temper tantrums and poor choices to dark moods and severe depressions.

From the moment I conceived my third child, a second daughter, she held a special place in my soul. In fact, during my pregnancy, she was tucked so deeply inside me that on the morning I arrived at the hospital knowing I was in labor, the attending nurse took one look at my flattened belly and suggested that I go home. Lying on the labor room bed and glancing down at my exposed toes, I too had to question, "Where is this baby?" But I knew in my soul that she was ready, waiting to claim a permanent place in my life and in my heart. Although her gender was yet a mystery, her spirit had been familiar from the very beginning.

I have often wondered whether every mother is gifted with clear memories concerning the birth of each of her children. I can still recall a commercial I viewed on television while my labor progressed, after the epidural, I might add. I'll never forget it, a Mormon commercial, one of those touchy-feely family-values ones. To the accompanying music of "Turn Around," a young mother was seen walking down a hospital corridor embracing a pink bundle. As she exited the hospital doors, escorted by the lyrics "Where are you going my little one, little one?" the woman turned around to glance back through the doors and, as if in a dream, glimpsed scenes of future events in her daughter's life.

*turn around and she's a little twirling ballerina,*
*turn around and she's prancing down the staircase in her*
    *prom dress,*
*turn around and she's walking down the aisle.*

With tears streaming down my cheeks, I found myself longing for another baby girl, well aware of how quickly those baby girls — and baby boys — grow up.

There was another member of our little family who was hoping for a girl. Three-and-a-half-year-old Megan had already chosen her sister's name just in case: Courtney. But when my baby was born a few hours later — weighing in at eight pounds, one and a half ounces, with a beautifully shaped head that sported soft black hair, a round face, and deep blue almond-shaped eyes — I knew she was an Emily. She seemed to confirm the choice the first time I held her in my arms. As I leaned down to softly whisper her name, she responded with a newborn grimace revealing a dimple in each cheek. I was in love with this beautiful baby.

Em, as we came to call her, brought great joy to our household. She seemed to know what to do with those dimples from infancy, often captivating people, always sharing her infectious laugh and being present to the life around her. When her dad lifted her out of the swimming pool after she had just won her heat in a swim meet when she was around six, her comment had been, "Dad, did you know that the sun and the moon are in the sky at the same time?" She had swum the backstroke oblivious to the competing swimmers in the adjacent lanes as well as to the loud cheers of all of us, her proud family, on the sideline.

At about age seven, Emily was among several students selected by her dancing instructor for the opening number of a dance revue — a ballet. Observing practice one day and captivated by the simple twirling of little ballerinas, I was caught off guard by an inner melody with familiar lyrics: "Turn around and she's a young girl." I swallowed hard to keep the tears from flowing and felt myself glancing back through those hospital doors.

Em's teenage years were less enchanting, complicated by a chain of losses beginning with my divorce when she was nine, the heartbreaking demolition of our family home for our city's economic progress, and my remarriage during her first year of college, not to mention the typical teenage losses and rejections. Each little death was dimming her light ever so gradually, until one day when she was about nineteen I could no longer deny that my once-vibrant expressive daughter was suffering and becoming enveloped by darkness. In fact, it suddenly dawned on me one day that the judgments I'd made of neglectful mothers over recent weeks were in fact my own shadow glaring back at me. It was time to examine my avoidance: Hadn't Em just gotten a speeding ticket and shown up recently looking disheveled to the point that I was uncomfortable in her presence? What part of me was denying the emotional outbursts, the empty laughter, the poor grades, the unfamiliar disposition as if a stranger had come to inhabit my beautiful daughter? My intuition was screaming: Something's wrong! Make yourself available. Go to her and find out the problem.

I wonder now about that courageous woman from Canaan, what her relationship with her daughter was like, how much they entrusted to one another. What kind of pain had her daughter endured to incite the woman to brave a daring confrontation? Had the woman been as afraid to hear the truth as I was on the fearsome day I confronted my daughter?

Emily and I spent the afternoon together at her college apartment examining her life. I was stunned to discover the depth of her pain and to embrace the reality of her depression. She admittedly expressed concern over some of the poor choices she had been making and acknowledged that she needed some help to sort it all out. I could hear that other desperate mother's words rising up from within me: "My daughter has a demon." In a way, that alarming admission spoken by a kindred spirit gave me hope: if her daughter could be healed, so could mine. Em's dad and I made the frightening decision to place her in a facility for evaluation, leading to a several-night stay. I was terrified, guilt-ridden, and incredibly sad. I needed the kind of courage and fortitude I imagined the Canaanite woman had.

Preparing to visit Emily the first evening was an ordeal. I was struggling with shame and fear, fighting an internal war between the opposing sides of feeling unfit as a mother and wanting to control my daughter's destiny. Before leaving my spiritual direction office, I scanned my bookshelves for my little travel Bible and every novena I could put my hands on. Righteously, I was clinging to the belief that if only she would pray and go to confession, her problems would go away. I was convinced I had the answers. I wonder now what answers my sister from Canaan thought she had before her remarkable day with Jesus. Surely she must have thought she alone knew what her daughter needed and, in fact, could handle her child's well-being.

That evening, seated at a table at the rehabilitation center among "family," which included my ex-husband, his wife, and three of my four children, I suffered the crushing blow that I had never expected my family to look like this. I felt like an outsider in a foreign land, perhaps like that pagan woman felt the day she voluntarily placed herself in the middle of strangers at Jesus's feet. And Jesus certainly appeared silent to me as he had to her in the midst of her trauma. Not that I was particularly looking for him.

Clutching tightly to my paper bag of religious goodies and looking for the perfect moment to slip them to her, I noticed her dad stretching across the table toward her. He handed Emily a carton of cigarettes, obviously the result of a phone conversation they'd had earlier. They grinned at each other, and I seethed inside. I hated him. I hated them all. I heard my son give his sister his big brotherly wisdom: "You just need to get your priorities together. That's all." I felt so alone, shamed as the Canaanite woman must have been, minus her vision and determination. I couldn't see through my own fears and judgments to grasp at the crumbs. I couldn't even think at that moment what the crumbs might be. The whole loaf seemed gone, shredded to bits in the chaos of destructive emotions within me. I hadn't a clue about where nourishment might come from for my aching heart.

It was my day off the next day, thank God. I needed to pray and I needed to cry, to weep in fact. I meditated on Matthew's Gospel about my soul sister from Canaan and felt the humiliation she must have experienced when Jesus called her a dog. It must have been a painful test. His seeming rejection didn't faze her, though. She knew what she wanted, and she wasn't going to give up. She wanted mercy, and she wanted the demon removed from her daughter.

There was yet another demon I was about to confront. This test felt like the weight of a final exam.

SITTING QUIETLY IN MY PRAYER CHAIR, I realized that the hatred in my heart was a call to go deep. I was still seething from my experience the night before, and I needed to examine myself a bit, to discover why I was so filled with rage and what about "them" was actually in me. Up to that point my only prayer had been, "Fix them, God." It's always so much easier to point the fingers outward. I prayed for courage and openness to look at myself and began to write in my journal. What was it about *them* that had enraged me?

I have discovered a freeing, yet sometimes agonizing exercise: listing the specific qualities in someone else that I find distasteful. My inventory that morning included arrogance and righteousness. I jotted down the grueling question: "What am *I* being righteous about?"

It felt good to write down the sources of my arrogance, a confession of sorts: that Em needed a religious experience for healing to take place, that her dad had been the cause of all her bad habits — most especially her smoking, that my holy, purer ways were better. It wasn't pretty.

As I scribbled down my virtuous opinions, I heard a rebuttal from deep inside, accompanied by a searing pain in my heart: *She didn't ask for the Bible. She asked for the cigarettes. Perhaps her dad is loving her better than you are.* Like a hundred-pound weight being lowered onto my chest, the discovery dawned that the demon was in me, the evil spirits of righteousness and arrogance and control. I prayed earnestly, "Lord, have mercy on me. Help me."

Pain erupted like a volcano exploding. I felt a surge of shame over the arrogance of being sure I knew what my daughter needed. I reflected painfully: Was my holier-than-thou attitude overcompensation for what I righteously believed her dad hadn't done for her? Had I put undue pressure on Em to be holy, as I defined holiness? Had I asked God what God wanted for her life?

I felt frustrated at having to continue to bear down on my own sinfulness. How much easier it had been to make it be about others. "Jesus, help me," I prayed. I begged for the grace to love Em as she was, to love them all, and to love myself. I prayed to surrender her healing and for the graces of trust, patience, and forgiveness that I needed to liberate not just myself, but also my daughter. I was the Canaanite woman, the determined pagan seeking relief and healing through my faith.

The most amazing thing happened on my next visit that very evening. Glancing around the same table looking at the identical faces, I felt love and I saw love in them, love that had been there the night before from which I had been blinded because of the log in my own eye.

Em's journey continues as does our shared one. Five years since that time, she has finished college, has just landed a new job, and is returning to that joyful child she always was. We work harder now to claim more time to spend together. I still find myself at times struggling with wanting her to do things my way. But I am trying hard to let go. Now I know that her holiness is a deep part of who she is and not dependent on what she does, nor on my criteria for holiness.

In glancing back on Matthew's account of "my story," I have come to realize that the woman's daughter was not the focus of her prayer. She sought mercy and help for herself. She certainly didn't lack faith that her daughter could be healed, but she was patient and perseverant in her prayer. The humility of Jesus's silence became a great gift. She went from demanding justice and begging for mercy, to surrendering herself and her daughter to God's care and love.

In facing my own self-righteousness, I was saved by grace. Difficult as it was to humble myself as the woman from Canaan had, I truly believe that when — in our weakness — we plead for Jesus's strength, we sometimes get much more than crumbs. We get the whole loaf — and Jesus might in fact say to us: "I like what I see. Your faith nourishes me. I can do nothing but respond to your great need. Be it done for you as you desire."

MY SISTER FROM CANAAN, your courage unleashed courage in me, helping me see that I too could face the demons and experience deep healing, not just for my daughter but indeed for myself. Thank you for showing me the way, for offering your own strength as a model for me to fight on. Pray for me if you would as I continue to face the challenges of mothering: to not give up when I mustn't, to ignore when I should, to love no matter what — and to never quit humbly praying, "Lord, help me."                                             — R.H.

# 6

# Sarah

## Why Can't I Have a Baby?

Now Sar'ai, Abram's wife, bore him no children.   — Genesis 16:1a

And God said to Abraham, "As for Sar'ai your wife, you shall not call her name Sar'ai, but Sarah shall be her name. I will bless her, and moreover I will give you a son by her; I will bless her, and she shall be a mother of nations; kings of peoples shall come from her."
— Genesis 17:15–16

God's infinite love is limited only by our need and hunger for his help. He has a reservoir of love that never runs out and that can be given only to the degree we have an empty vessel because we know our weakness and need.
— Dennis and Matthew Linn, *Healing Life's Hurts*

**LHD** I feel a deep kinship with the woman Sarah and her long and painful struggle to have a child.

The first twelve years of my married life were a struggle with infertility. When I had not conceived after a year, I began medical tests, taking my temperature and enduring many other indignities in order to become pregnant.

My quest was punctuated by an exclamation of joy, when my son, Jacques, was born in 1976 after four years of treatment. I was the happiest pregnant woman ever, and surely Jacques was the most loved and longed-for child on the face of the earth. (Well, that's the way *I* felt.) He was a perfect, healthy baby. So, you ask, what happened? Why are you, Lyn, writing about your infertility now?

I wonder about this sometimes, myself. I very much wanted a second child. Was I selfish to want more children, was I greedy, when so many other women struggled and never conceived, even once? Perhaps. I just wanted another baby; I wanted a sibling for Jacques and another child for my husband, Dee, and me to love.

My doctors told us to try again soon after Jacques's birth, and that was fine with us. They assured me that there was no reason why I wouldn't conceive again. When I didn't, after a few years, I had surgery and took more drugs. At times back then, I felt as though infertility ruled my life and took over all my thoughts and feelings. Yet I never got pregnant again.

So I was deeply drawn to Sarah (her name was Sarai before she conceived) because I knew about her suffering and the deep desire to have a child. However, I thought our theologies were very different, before I delved more deeply into my memories of trying to conceive. I knew from my studies of the Bible that the Hebrew people in Sarai's time had a simple, rather black-and-white faith. Everything — good and bad — came directly from the hand of their God, through God's active decision. They didn't consider secondary causes (like endometriosis, which I had) and knew little about science. Therefore, rain, rich harvests, and children were gifts from God's hand, and disease, famine, and sterility were punishments for sin from the very same God. I believed that Sarai would have understood her childlessness as a sure sign that God had turned away from her and no longer loved her, through her own fault. I was surprised when I revisited my own memories of infertility and realized that I had felt much the same way.

The truth is that when I was struggling with this problem, I held a suppressed feeling of failure deep within me, like a chronic low-grade fever. Barely conscious were feelings that I must have done *something* wrong. Was I too thin? Too stressed? Was it those times I drank too much? Didn't eat right? Was I too emotional, too unfeminine, too — something? The tests showed it *was* some physical problem I had, eventually diagnosed as endometriosis, and not my husband's problem. This confirmed some of my negative thoughts.

I experienced God at this time as very far away and much removed from my suffering. For some reason, I embraced an image of a busy, male God who was fed up with my whining and had more important things on his mind than babies. And I embraced that hurtful image not really knowing that I had done so.

Sarai, ah, Sarai. I know a lot about what you went through. You lived in a harsher, more patriarchal culture than I, in which a woman earned her worth by having children. Your whole sense of yourself as a good wife, helpmate, and godly person would have been severely compromised by your infertility. It is odd to confess that my whole sense of self was compromised too. Even though my husband never said a negative word to me, and was thrilled with one child, there was still a wound in my womanhood, a hurting place. Sometimes I was filled with darkness. At times, I was rude to others who seemed to have children with great ease. I can comprehend your cruelty, my ancient friend, even your sending your maid-servant and her child out into the wilderness when despair darkened your vision and clouded your judgment. I under-stand, because my own suffering, rather than increasing my spirituality, threatened to destroy the little I had.

As the years passed, I usually managed my disappointment well, and more and more I tried to remove it from my daily thoughts. Then, when my son was twelve, my best friend got pregnant for the second time after her own struggles with con-ceiving. I descended into angry depression and despair for several months. I didn't know that my suffering was about to take a U-turn, and that my greatest grief would be the catalyst for my deepest joy.

One evening I lay on my bed crying and reading a book called *Paying Attention to God,* by Jesuit priest William Barry. In the book, the author advised the reader to tell God every-thing, being perfectly honest, and even expressing deep anger. I decided to follow this course, as nothing else had worked.

I wept harder, pouring out my anger and frustration at God. I told him that he was a beast for withholding another child from me, that I was a good mother. A good mother! And Dee was a great father, and a child would find a very happy home with us.

Suddenly, without warning, I was plunged into a deep, feath-ery, gray darkness, and I experienced what I can only call an altered state of consciousness. I was encased in a darkness that had weight, depth, and texture as though I had fallen down a rabbit hole, so to speak. I was unable to see anything around me. Time stopped or had no meaning; I guess I was in a sort of shadowy yet sweet "swoon." That is as close as I can come to describing my altered state. While I was in this heavenly place, I heard words spoken in a voice like the sea, a voice from deep within the earth, or the heavens, a rich, warm voice that I audibly heard, which said, "I love your Lyn-ness."

After these words were spoken, the darkness evaporated. I don't know how much time passed before I became myself again, but changed. I was left to shakily ponder the experience and the strange words "I love your Lyn-ness." What could that mean? As I savored the experience, scarcely able to believe it, I was filled with the most intense state of peace, love, and joy that I have ever experienced. The distinctive graces of this wonderful state lasted, richly present and very real, for three full days, and when they quietly dissipated, they left a great sense of peace in my soul.

It took many months, even years, to dissect this message. I feel now that God was telling me that he loved my essence, my very core, the *who* of who I was, my Lyn-ness. It was a deep and wonderful message of unconditional love. Here was a God who did not need more children from me to love me completely. From that day forth, I knew there was a loving God, even when I did not understand God's ways. I began to forget about wanting more children and to treasure what I had, as I reached out for more and more spiritual growth and experiences. Like Sarai's name changing to Sarah, when I heard the words "I love your Lyn-ness," it was as though *my* name was changed. My name was changed to *Beloved.*

*What was it like for you, Sarai? When your name was changed? Was there a blaze of light, whispers inside you, things you never shared aloud? Did God reach down to you and pull you deep into whispery darkness, enfold you in love, speak love to your very heart?*

Because of this experience, I no longer see God as a puppet master who gives or withholds the things we want. I see God as the source of all life and the ground of our being. Father Thomas Keating asks, "Is God just as present in absence as in presence? Or to put it another way, Is the divine intervention always there supporting us whether we think it is present or not?" I would say yes and add that it is the very fact that we do not understand God's ways that calls for faith. Perfect understanding would require no faith at all.

Another gift of this journey is that I came face to face with my sense of entitlement. Like Sarai, at some level I believed that if I strove to do everything right, I would get everything I wanted. It seems ridiculous to even write this now. I had closed my eyes to the suffering of so many innocent people in this world, and it was time for me to grow in wisdom. It was time to learn that *all* life was gift, from the first breath to the last — pure gift — and that I wasn't entitled to any of it.

Today I have many reasons to believe that, whether four thousand years ago or in our present day, the struggles of women are close to God's heart. Perhaps this is the very reason that the Holy Spirit has brought the compelling story of Sarai/Sarah to us across the bridge of thousands of years and many, many miles. Like her we can learn that we are not abandoned, even in — especially in — our suffering. Never abandoned, but deeply, deeply loved.              — L.H.D.

## SARAH

When I left my father's lands deep within the richest
   valley,
My beauty was well-known, my laughter medicine to the
   ear.
I was a thousand silver bells upon a misty hillside,
A hundred tent flags red beneath the sun.
I came to you, my love, I laughed with joy beside you,
Bearing gifts to make a husband proud.

For I would be a watered tree, bearing fruit in every
   season,
Beloved of God and man, I would be filled. For I did all
   things
Righteously, observing every law.
God rewards the righteous and I was.
I was. But others gained what I was never given,
My roots began to dry in endless sun.

I prayed on mountaintops and deep within the walls of
   holy places,
I looked for God in sun-streaked skies and behind the
   temple walls.
Silence was in the mountains, I was just a woman; God,
   you didn't love me!
I only heard a word, or maybe two,
*It is not to be and not for you.*

I drank the blood-red juice bought dear from one old
   woman.
Her cave-like house sat at the city gates,

She ground her herbs, and they were caustic, sour,
    fragrant.
Days later I would tear my hair and weep.

And still at night you pulled me close and told me of your
    visions. You held them tight against the crushing
Loss. You spoke of stars that gathered high within the
    heavens, told your fortune — you said,
It won't end this way. For in a smoldering firepot God has
    shown me hope,
I think I see the problem now. Your wife has not found
    favor, is rejected,
Is lost within the black and smoldering smoke.

And when my heart had turned to charcoal, we
Used a servant girl for our own ends. I gave with one
    hand, took back with another,
The gift I gave you threw me into rage; I
Sent them off to die one darkening day.
You saved her, God; was she the one you loved?
I had no hope of mercy, now, within your touch.

Soon sunrise meant no more than brittle heat,
And bread that never rose beneath my barren hands.
I loved you; you loved me, that made it worse.
The tents were soft as butter now, I rolled our own,
And longed for water deep within a foreign land.

There was nothing left for me but tending fires and
    weaving wool,
until I saw a desert hare dead still upon a golden rock,

And heard a whoosh of silence that bore much and made
    me turn
To see the three of them so near with robes of startling
    white.
They bowed and entered in, my bread rose up so high
    and light.

And quail splashed high into a pale and northern sky,
And rain sailed by before it touched earth,
And one small deer got caught within our tented walls,
And silver bells were heard upon the hills.

And much was made of me and my first words to them,
I said I didn't laugh; it wasn't true of course.
They thought that I was frivolous, an unbelieving wench,
And were quick content to leave me to my fires and
    rolled-up tents.
Perhaps they even wondered at the ways of God,
To send a special boy child to a crone so odd.

Ah — none could see I laughed because I knew it was all
    true.
I long forgave them, what do angels feel?
They only brought the message, perhaps they couldn't
    know,
That butter-soft and wrinkled deep, my face was kissed
    by life,
As vivid as a hundred flags blood-red upon the hills.
I laughed because the God of women lived, forgave,
And loved me still.                —L.H.D.

# 7

# Mary Magdalene

## It's Time for Me to Let Go

Jesus said to her, "Woman, why are you weeping? For whom are you looking?" Supposing him to be the gardener, she said to him, "Sir, if you have carried him away, tell me where you have laid him, and I will take him away." Jesus said to her, "Mary!" She turned and said to him in Hebrew, "Rabbouni!" (which means Teacher). Jesus said to her, "Stop holding on to me, because I have not yet ascended to the Father. But go to my brothers and say to them, 'I am ascending to my Father and your Father, to my God and your God.'" Mary Magdalene went and announced to the disciples, "I have seen the Lord," and she told them that he had said these things to her.

— John 20:15–18

When Jesus calls her by name, an unheard of liberation and change takes place in Mary Magdalene. She experiences the complete and radical transition into a new life that stands before her in the person of Jesus and is given to her through him. She receives her name — and herself — completely renewed.

— Peter van Breemen, S.J., *The God Who Won't Let Go*

RH     I always believed that Mary Magdalene was the Gospel prostitute. Then when I traveled to the Holy Land several years ago, it was liberating to hear our guide introduce her more likely profession: merchant, a career few women enjoyed at the time of Jesus, a choice that made her a threat to her peers. Imagining her as a businesswoman made so much more sense to me, as she was among those impassioned women who tended to Jesus out of their own resources, funds she would have obtained through her business. It seemed to me, then, that the "seven demons" Jesus supposedly cured her of could have been my own: greed, selfishness, control, pride, jealousy, anger, and fear — those demons to which I can more easily relate than the struggles of prostitution.

As I've reread the Scriptures that contain elements of her story, I have come to know her better. I really like her spirit, her stick-to-itiveness, her fierce loyalty, her passion. She gives me the courage to keep my heart open during the worst of times, to bear down on the pain of loss, to hang in long after others have gone home, and yes, to let go in love, something that has never been easy for me.

I remember a time in my own life when an encounter with Jesus, disguised as a woman on an airplane, was akin to Mary Magdalene's encounter with Jesus, masked as a gardener. Mine took place as I stood peering into the empty tomb of my marriage, wondering where it had been laid. I was clearly being issued an invitation into a new life as Mary had been in the garden by Jesus's tomb.

I don't know whether there were symbols in Mary Magdalene's life that enabled her to awaken, but in my life the symbol of a bird would become a sacred invitation to break free. The symbol's inaugural appearance occurred innocently one morning — when a brown thrasher flew in front of my car. This probably happened often, but on that day I took notice.

And then the phenomenon took off, while on a lonely excursion to a friend's beach house in Galveston, Texas, one cold January. My husband and I had been separated for over a year, and I had begged him to join me on this trip, thinking that if we could just spend time together alone, we could sort out our struggles. When he refused, I knew I needed to go anyway to begin to sort out my own. It was overwhelming to consider a future without him.

The hungry seagulls encircling the Galveston Bay ferry, the shorebirds, and one tall egret on the beach were my solitary companions for those lonesome, reflective days. They taught me a great deal about grace and stillness, trust and beauty. Sitting on the deck overlooking the Gulf one sunny morning, I observed the elegant gulls gliding with outstretched wings on the currents of a brisk January breeze. I pondered their freedom and wrote in my journal that they seemed to be telling me that it was my time to soar.

When I returned home, a frightened bird greeted me in my kitchen. He had entered through the open chimney flue and had been forced to wait until I got home and could offer him release. In the weeks that followed, a mother chimney swift decided to build her nest in the fireplace chimney in my bedroom. Each morning around 5:30, I was awakened by her noisy efforts to feed her babies. I came to enjoy the rustling sounds as she flew up and down the chimney and can still hear the peeping of her babies as they anticipated her return. That mother bird became my soul companion that spring, and I looked forward to the sound of her presence. She made my mundane and now lonely task of feeding hungry little mouths sacramental as we arose together to begin our days.

One March morning while I was on my daily walk, the sound of a bird overhead caught my attention. Beyond the bird many miles away was a jet. Glancing high above the clouds at that

soaring airplane, my soul stirred with a yearning to travel somewhere, anywhere, just to give my spirit something to look
forward to. Listening intently to my heart, an idea arose about
a summer workshop with Mary Elizabeth Marlow, a personal
mentor. The retreat would take place on a Greek island the
upcoming June, and it was entitled "Phoenix Rising: Stepping
beyond Your Limitations." (It took a year for me to notice the
profound synchronicity of the title, as I truly didn't think at the
time about the phoenix being a bird!) I didn't have a lot of extra
financial resources, but when I got home from my walk, I called
Mary Elizabeth and asked her to hold me a spot. I was going to
Greece.

I knew this trip would be a new beginning for me. I thought
of it as a honeymoon with myself. I yearned to step beyond the
fear and sadness that had settled over my spirit the last twenty
months or so and to bring healing and joy into my life and my
children's lives. We all deserved much more than the grief that
had saturated our household like a frigid rainy winter that never
seems to end.

By the time my June departure day rolled around, my spirit
was ripe and open. Like Mary Magdalene, I was perseverant in
my search for the holy. She must have felt very alone, as I did
during that time of my life. The empty tombs we both faced
were opportunities to recognize that God is much greater than
can be imagined.

Boarding the enormous plane, I found my seat in the middle
section of the craft amid people of various nationalities. Though
I was traveling alone, I felt blessed with a much-needed and
unusual sense of connectedness. I didn't feel lonely at all. Here
I was, a brokenhearted single woman about to take off to a

frightfully uncertain future, yet I was filled with eagerness and anticipation.

Sitting patiently in my seat observing the multitudes enter the airplane, I noticed the woman who would become my travel companion move into my aisle and attempt to place her luggage over and under the seat next to mine, as good air travelers should. She couldn't seem to get her overnight bag placed under the seat in front of her, so I reached down to help, slipping it in easily. I stood to greet her.

She spoke gently and lovingly, "Why, you're an angel."

I felt an energy in her statement and an inner declaration from deep within: "Pay attention," the voice murmured.

"What's your name?" the woman asked.

"Robin," I responded, feeling excited to meet a new friend.

And then the prophetess spoke, the Jesus in disguise who would provide the impetus for a resounding yes uttered from my soul: *"Robin*. Like a bird, you're getting ready to fly. No, like your name, you're getting ready to soar." My plane hadn't even lifted off from the runway in Dallas, and here was a woman from Vienna, Austria, synthesizing my experiences of the last several months and foretelling that my own resurrection was imminent. I knew I was on holy ground. Like Mary Magdalene, I had found a seed of hope in a trusted friend.

Serena and I spent our trans-Atlantic trip sharing thoughts between naps. I told her my story and shared the longing that had brought me to that place in time, the desire to end my struggle with clinging to a husband who had clearly begun a new life. Even in that moment I was still holding steadily to the notion of family as I had always known it. She offered me courage and a new mission with this profound thought: "So you've been a wife and a mother, and now it's time to get back to the Source again."

Serena became my rabbouni, my teacher. And although she didn't firmly admonish me to stop holding on as Jesus had reprimanded his student, she did offer a gentle invitation to relax my hold on those familiar roles of wife and mother. God, the Source, had much more to give me if I would just let go. As we parted ways, Serena looked me straight in the eyes and exclaimed, "I can just see you fly — like a robin. Have a beautiful life. A fruitful life." I departed the airplane knowing I was clearly in new territory and not just in a different country.

That pilgrimage to Greece initiated my new life. The entire experience that began months before with the flight of a little bird was the threshold for stepping beyond the self-imposed limitations brought on by my persistent clinging. I was to return home to begin a new relationship with the Spirit within and to face with courage the challenging changes ahead.

MARY MAGDALENE, what a beautiful path you walked — a path that unfolded with a holy desire, a chance encounter, a spoken name, an empty tomb, a statement of empowerment, and a new life — all the elements of that scene in Jerusalem that joined together once again in another solitary woman's journey two thousand years later.

You, too, heard your name called and were told to stop holding on. You had made Jesus as you knew him your God. I had made marriage and family as I knew them my God. You were awakened to a new life and walked forward from your pilgrimage to the tomb with a new vision, a new vocation as apostle to the apostles, fortified by his Spirit within you. I walked forward with new dreams, secured by the amazing strength I received by his presence on my holy pilgrimage to Greece.

From our privileged encounters, we both learned the most important lesson of our lives: that possessiveness and love are not synonymous. Each of us came to understand that the purified love gained through enduring much pain offers the fuel for mission, as it calls us out of ourselves and into the larger world of compassion and service. We learned that the Kingdom of God had been in us both all along. As I write this now, our hard-earned wisdom reminds me still, "Let go of what you've known. Stop clinging to people, things, and opinions. Let go, so you can have a beautiful and, yes, a fruitful life. Let go."

—R.H.

# 8

# Mary of Magdala

## Da Vinci, Ya Never Knew Me

Soon afterward he went on through cities and villages, preaching and bringing the good news of the kingdom of God. And the twelve were with him, and also some women who had been healed of evil spirits and infirmities: Mary, called Magdalene, from whom seven demons had gone out, and Joanna, the wife of Chuza, Herod's steward, and Susanna, and many others, who provided for them out of their means.                         —Luke 8:1–3

"He is not here, he has risen! Remember how he told you, while he was still in Galilee, that the Son of man must be delivered into the hands of sinful men, and be crucified, and on the third day rise."

And they remembered his words, and returning from the tomb they told all this to the eleven and to all the rest. Now it was Mary Magdalene and Joanna and Mary the mother of James and the other women with them who told this to the apostles.     —Luke 24:6–10

That Jesus welcomed female disciples into his entourage was highly unusual, since Jewish men normally didn't speak to women outside of their families in public, much less allow them to travel around the countryside with them. Women's equal call to discipleship is perhaps most evident in the Resurrection account, for it is upon the testimony of women that the proclamation of the resurrection depends. All four Gospels show Mary of Magdala, Joanna, Mary the mother of James and Joses, Salome and other women disciples accompanying Jesus to his death; anointing and burying his body, viewing the empty tomb; and finally experiencing his risen presence.
—Ute Eisen and Dorothy Irvin, as quoted in
*Women Officeholders in the Early Church*,
compiled by FutureChurch

**LHD** I stared at the black and gray drawing of Mary of Magdala on the front of the FutureChurch brochure that had just arrived in the mail. I always visualized Mary Magdalene with red hair. *That can't be right*, I said to myself, staring at her upraised hands, her open female gaze as depicted in this appealing drawing by Verlaj. *She would have been dark haired with olive skin, surely.* Maybe I had seen a painting somewhere depicting her with red hair. Maybe I wanted her hair to be red like mine, for the more I learned about her, the more I liked her.

I went over what I now believed I knew about her. First of all, there was *no* biblical evidence that she was a prostitute. Scholars disagree about how this image of her has arisen, and scholarly explanations ranged from the benign to the sinister. On the one hand, she might have just been confused with the "woman who loved much" in Luke 7:36–50, a woman with a bad reputation who washed Jesus's feet with her tears. On the other hand, there might be a conspiracy against her. Mary M. was a strong apostolic woman and some people in the years after her death were threatened by this and stole her power by distorting the truth about her. In either case or both, the final effect was the same: it is generally accepted by New Testament scholars that Mary Magdalene is a maligned, underestimated, and misunderstood — yet central — figure in New Testament accounts of Jesus's ministry.

She *was* a strong apostolic woman; about this there can be little doubt. There is evidence that she and other women traveled with Jesus and the disciples as he ministered and preached. Mary was one of few people who remained at the foot of the cross during Jesus's agonizing death, and she was the first person to whom he appeared when he arose. I paused to think about this fact for a moment. *Suppose a man whom I and others loved deeply has died. Then, in some wonderful way, he has conquered death and has appeared to me before appearing to any other.* I let this idea sink in. What would this appearance say about this man's affection and regard for me? I am filled with wonder and excitement when I meditate on this scenario. Ah, Jesus, how you care for us and how you love Mary Magdalene!

How much clearer a message could Christ have left about how important Mary Magdalene was to him and to the Christian faith? This Easter appearance to Mary of Magdala is reported in all four Gospel accounts, and few scholars doubt its basis in fact.

The brochure I was holding described Mary as "a strong woman." I remembered a time when those words were said about me. Twenty years ago my dear friend Yvette, during a routine conversation, said to me matter-of-factly, "Well, Lyn, you are such a *strong* woman, you know." I recall my reaction, and it was not one of joy but of chagrin. Thinking back on this conversation, I realized that what I had heard on some level was, "Lyn, you are filled with animus; you are insensitive." But that was not what my friend had said. She only said that I was "strong." I know now that strong women get good things done. Strong women endure and prosper and bring hope into their homes and other people's lives. Why couldn't I embrace the word "strong" back then?

During this same time period my friend, Dale, was talking about a seminar he had attended where he had learned about the cultivation and use of power. "Power!" I said disapprovingly,

"We're supposed to be tender and surrendering, not filled with power!" He looked at me keenly and said softly, "Lyn, do you think the only kind of power is evil power?" I guess I did. I guess I thought that power in the hands of mere humans was always evil. It is so easy to misunderstand the Gospel message and to feel that women are supposed to cultivate passivity and surrender excessively, causing us to overadapt to others at the risk of our own mental health. Assertiveness and the cultivation of a clear vision for one's life-call are Gospel virtues, as demonstrated by Mary of Magdala. No one could keep her away from Jesus's cross or his tomb. Clearly, she followed the Lord despite fear and threatening obstacles. "Gosh," I thought. "I hope that young Christian women can hear more about the story of Mary Magdalene and that it will encourage them to remain in their faith and follow her example."

I shook away these thoughts and sat at the computer to search the Internet for information about Mary M. Thousands of sites came up, many with the book *The Da Vinci Code* attached. Soon I was gazing at portraits of her with red hair. *Of course,* I thought, *she is often portrayed this way; it is illustrative of her passion.* For this is another aspect of Mary M. that has made many Christians uncomfortable: the passion in this life bleeds through the Gospel stories and cannot help but be noticed. Her passionate vigil at the cross. Her passionate waiting at the tomb. She loved him; she really did, and she never turned away for a moment. She was quite a woman.

But there is no evidence that she was married to him or involved with Jesus in that way. Had she been, she would have been called "Mary, the wife of Jesus," and in these ancient Jewish texts this wouldn't have been scandalous. Jewish prophets and healers did not have to be single men and, in fact, usually they were married. However, biblical evidence indicates strongly that Jesus never married.

Mary of Magdala was not identified with any male, a most unusual condition for a female of her time. She was an independent woman, and because of her unusual designation as Mary of Magdala — Magdala denoting her city of origin — all indications are that this Mary belonged to herself and to God alone. And because she did, she could give her heart to Jesus freely.

But, you may ask, wasn't she rather crazy? Didn't Jesus have to cast seven demons out of her?

Yes, Jesus did. But the scholars say this only indicates that Mary of Magdala was ill and that Jesus healed her. The number seven was used to denote a serious illness, or perhaps one illness with many symptoms; there is no evidence that her illness was a mental illness. The use of the word *demon* did not have the connotation that it does today.

Was she grateful to Jesus for healing her? I believe she was. But her faithfulness went far beyond gratitude. Mary of Magdala became one of Jesus's apostles. She was a disciple. She supported Jesus with her own financial resources (Luke 8:1–3). She believed that his message could save the world, and she risked her own safety and good name as she traveled with Jesus and his disciples and as she stood bravely by the cross and at the tomb. When I consider this rich and wonderful story of Mary of Magdala, my heart is filled with joy, and I want to pray for new ways of being.

And so for what do I pray? I hope for changes in my own heart as I continue to walk in meditation with Mary Magdalene.

She showed the kind of strength and passion that I want to display in my own life. I want to be respectful of authority, but not fearful of it. I want to listen daily as God speaks within my own heart. Then I can learn to be courageous enough to share my inner truth with love. Perhaps sometimes, like Mary Magdalene was, I will be misunderstood. This can be so painful to a woman like me who is accustomed to pleasing people and having them like her. But perhaps being true to God as I have *experienced* God, despite the uncertain response of others, is simply another phase of growing up and becoming more perfected as Jesus asked us to.

When I can be strong in this feminine way, I can bring hope to our broken world. This hurting world is, I believe, crying out for the compassion, collaboration, creativity, and peace that come from the feminine soul. We women can offer a new vision of the Gospel, a vision that can bring balance to a world driven by competition and violence. I know in my heart that our prayers and our gifts can bring healing and restoration as we follow our Lord.

And so finally, I pray for women all around the world to stand tall as I feel Mary Magdalene did, and to experience the deep sense of self-esteem that comes when we know we are truly loved by God. In this love we can live in brother-sisterhood in our homes, our churches, our communities, and our world.

We can follow the example of Mary Magdalene, no greater sinner than any of us. She was a woman among many whom Jesus touched with empowerment and grace. Yes, Jesus, who makes all things new, loves and values the souls of women deeply. And they responded to him with love, loyalty, and service on the pages of the Gospels. When we hear about how women were Jesus's disciples and his apostles, we can reframe a vision of our roles as women in the church today.

God gifted Mary Magdalene with unwavering loyalty and strength, gifts that have brought her true story all the way down through the centuries to us today. Hers is a story that will not die. I think, my dear friends, that she *may* have been a feisty redhead, not unheard of in Israel. And she was a woman surely, whom Jesus accepted in all her strength, her independence, and her passion as well as her weaknesses. She was a woman, like us, who loved Jesus. And she was a woman, like us, whom Jesus loved.                                    —L.H.D.

## MARY OF MAGDALA

Magdala,
In the landscape of my prayer,
We laughed together, you and I,
After the wine had grown thick in the cup
And the fire folded in, all chalk and spark.
You said,
"What do you think of him? Did you ever know a man
        such as he?"
I sat, raw from the winds of the day and chilled in the
        wine-cold air,
Lost in thoughts that rushed and burned and swirled.

I turned to see your fierce brown eyes seek mine (you
        waited, would not turn away),
and slowly I replied,
"I never knew a man like him, and yes I see,
What you have tried to tell me these long days.

My heart has come alive within me and I will ask,
Can I come with you now? Never leave you now?"
I am rewarded with your smile.

Magdala, then I walked with you and him
And all the others,
You taught me to bake bread on hot and
Smoothed-out rocks,
At the edges of villages, where
People thronged to see his face.
We saw the healings, heard the cries of joy.
We cried together,
Praising God and breaking bread with wonder. Sisters,
Holding gently what each day brought forth.

Yet even we heard power as it
Called forth streams of darkness,
That sought to douse the healing light within his touch.

He sought your counsel when decisions
Came each day,
He listened keenly as you spoke,
And you did listen well to him.
I heard you pray together on the hills, beside the rivers.
He told you things perhaps he told no others.

I had not seen respect
Shown to a Hebrew woman in *this* way,
I wondered when you met him,
How it all had come to be,
But certain things you would not speak, remained a
    mystery.

Days passed,
I brushed your auburn hair and plaited it tight for you,
    deep within valleys of green olives,
Where purple clouds of grapes
grew near the tiny streams that brought us life.
You spoke your passion, "I never knew
One
who cared about the poor the way he does,
There are so many!
He works so hard to make the sick be healed, the
    burdened free.
This is the love, the love he gives to me.
He makes me care for little ones, and ah — he makes me
    love them,
I never knew what love was till he came,
Will never know such healing love again."

You laughed then sadly, holding back your tears,
For words are cheap and cannot say the things we know.
You wrapped your linen robes around you
At the coming of the night,
Within the women's tent, you washed my feet so gently,
Told me of your fear
That they would surely kill him in the end.

"This world can be no friend," you said, with tears at last,
    that would not stay within your amber eyes,
But slowly watered first your mouth, then breast.
"Can be no friend," you took my hand
And laid it on your chest,
"Can be no friend of
His, the perfect heart."        —L.H.D.

# 9

# The Prodigal Daughter

## I Want to Go Home

Then Jesus said, "There was a man who had two sons. The younger of them said to his father, 'Father, give me the share of the property that will belong to me.' So he divided his property between them. A few days later the younger son gathered all he had and traveled to a distant country, and there he squandered his property in dissolute living. When he had spent everything, a severe famine took place throughout that country, and he began to be in need. . . . But when he came to himself he said, 'How many of my father's hired hands have bread enough and to spare, but here I am dying of hunger! I will get up and go to my father, and I will say to him, "Father, I have sinned against heaven and before you; I am no longer worthy to be called your son; treat me like one of your hired hands.' " So he set off and went to his father. . . . And they began to celebrate."
—Luke 15:11–14, 17–20a, 24

Leaving home is, then, much more than an historical event bound to time and place. It is a denial of the spiritual reality that I belong to God with every part of my being, that God holds me safe in an eternal embrace, that I am indeed carved in the palm of God's hands and hidden in their shadows. Leaving home means ignoring the truth that God has "fashioned me in secret, moulded me in the depths of the earth and knitted me together in my mother's womb." Leaving home is living as though I do not yet have a home and must look far and wide to find one. —Henri Nouwen, *The Return of the Prodigal Son*

The call from God is to come home, to embrace both our littleness and our greatness and come home. Come home to our families, our friends, our church, our selves, our God.
—Macrina Wiederkehr, *A Tree Full of Angels*

RH    There is a sculpture at my friend Deanna's home that caught my eye many years ago. The striking image is a small clay rendering of the prodigal son, only swaddled in the arms of the father is not a young man, but instead his daughter, held close by large embracing hands. The first time I glimpsed the stirring sculpture, it dawned on me that there is of course a female counterpart to the story that some say is the heart of the Gospel. It is not only sons who leave home and squander their inheritance. Both daughters and sons do some of the oddest things in an attempt to disown the reality that they belong to God. Glancing at that sculpture, I saw myself kneeling before my Father, seeking to remember my divine identity, to be at home in his eternal embrace.

Reflecting on the compelling Gospel story surrounding that moving visual of the eternal homecoming, I recognized an internal resonance with the prodigal one's struggles — the troubles we all undergo when we move away from our true selves, following our own wills and stubborn natures to a distant country. Like the adult child in Luke's Gospel, I have often lived selfishly, spending my energy trying to please everyone but the One I should please, and looking for love in very remote places. These struggles began in my childhood, just as I imagine they did for the prodigal one long before that journey back home.

I grew up in New Orleans, the youngest of three in a family that lacked a strong sense of connectedness. My dad's sudden and tragic death when I was ten years old weakened our family nucleus, and we each took on roles typical of a family broken by suffering. My mother's natural overprotection enabled me to opt for the Neverland of childhood, clinging to the stance of *puella* — the eternal girl who tenaciously holds onto the apron strings of comfort and outer security. I let my mother fight my battles, and I depended on her strength. I also adored her. She doted on me, spoiled me in many ways, and suffered my pain for me.

Mamma's seeming favoritism understandably gnawed at my brother and sister, the elders in my story, the two members of my family who never quite understood me. Theirs was an exclusive relationship that they had enjoyed for several years before I came along; their close bond was not meant to oust me. Of that I'm sure. Nevertheless, I was the child who was teased as being adopted, the one who didn't appear with the others in the lovely photo (because I hadn't been born yet!) that sat on my daddy's dresser. Somehow the adorable picture suggested that I just didn't fit in — so while they were enjoying the natural connection of a brother and sister, I was creating imaginary friends. During our growing-up years, we drifted further apart, their alliance gaining strength as my need for belonging was sought elsewhere. I buried myself in an unhealthy relationship with my high school boyfriend, a relationship that was emotionally abusive. I clung to him for years, finally breaking it off when the new life of college summoned a fresh start.

My mother's remarriage when I was a college sophomore, prompting the sale of our family home and her move to Missouri, left my spirit dangling in thin air. I had lost my home, and I had also lost my center, the maternal security that had sustained me all of my life. I was the one to transport my mom and brand-new stepfather to the airport, to see them off on their new life together, and to sit alone in a chair at the terminal gate after they had boarded the plane, aching with loneliness. My loss that morning reopened the wound left by my dad's death, the pain of abandonment that often pulsed and occasionally hemorrhaged, as it did that day in the airport. It would take me a long time to discover that both losses were a necessary part of my journey, a journey into adulthood that would involve a long, meandering trek into distant country — moving away from familiar roots, and traveling to faraway places in search of my feminine nature, my true self.

Glancing back at the Gospel story, I imagine the many ways that we prodigal ones dissipate our energies, our chronic efforts to seek external comfort as a means of deadening the fears that inhabit our spirits. These attempts to fill our aching hearts are often not immoral, as we sometimes imagine the Scripture character's were, but are nonetheless destructive to our souls. My deep fear of abandonment would keep me imprisoned in chronic codependency for a long time. It was a wound that could never be healed, never be restored to health, in the arms of anyone but God. In my early twenties, I was far from that awareness.

Only six days after that dismal trip to the airport, I met my future husband. I chuckle now when I think of his name, Brother. *Ah, family,* I must have thought, standing on a ski slope in Crested Butte, Colorado, on a college-sponsored ski trip. Brother seemed to encapsulate the familiar traits of my family: wit, confidence, a sense of fun, pride. I needed a place to belong. He seemed to fit the bill. As in any courtship based on neediness, there would be obvious limitations and problems. All I knew was a desperate need to be loved and to belong to another. He too had lost his dad during adolescence, and in many ways we were both in search of fathers, both prodigal children in search of a home. I believed with all my heart that marriage would make me complete. I wanted it more than anything in the world.

Our fifteen-year marriage was altogether blessed and pain-filled, graced by four beautiful children, but limited by awkward attempts to nurture a covenant that was being lived out in the distant land of selfishness and immaturity. Neither of us had fully grown up into our adult selves, but we both tried hard to love well. Beneath my chronic struggles with busyness, control, distractedness, and dissatisfaction was a deep longing for God, a longing I couldn't seem to access, although I did seek God in community, the Cursillo movement, and Theresians. I prayed often for grace — for healing and peace.

With many prodigals, it is pain and suffering that prompt our journeys home. The Gospel infers that starvation induced the prodigal's return, along with the sudden realization that his inherent riches had been scattered, that God's glory had been recklessly forgotten. My own prompting came as another hemorrhaging wound, when I faced the task of letting go of the life I had clamored for, the one I had latched onto for security and belonging.

Facing the devastating blow of divorce, I had to confront head-on my selfishness, my clinging nature, and the chronic dissatisfaction with which I often approached my life. I was forced to look at evidence in my life of times when I just didn't love well, when my focus was on meeting my own needs and not the needs of my loved ones, much less the needs of my Beloved. I traveled to those places within myself where I was imprisoned by fear and began my journey home. It was time to discover True Love. Many guides and several spiritual directors led the way.

Father Henri Nouwen became for me, as he has for so many readers, a spiritual father, offering an adult world that was approachable and even desirable. He too had suffered with issues of damaged self-esteem, outwardly admitting through countless writings his struggles with seeking love in faraway places. The first time I read his *The Return of the Prodigal Son,* I was mesmerized. It was the most moving book I'd ever read. The entire text is based on Rembrandt's painting by the same name, which Nouwen viewed in St. Petersburg, Russia. The picture stirred Nouwen's soul deeply, and his feelings spilled over the pages he wrote. In his typically vulnerable and passionate approach, Nouwen transported the reader into the story of the prodigal one.*

My first reading incited a longing for healing. I identified with the prodigal, with the homelessness and fatigue inherent in living far away from my center, from God. I too had spent much of my life disregarding the soft whisper that calls me beloved, listening instead to the louder and more seductive voices of power, popularity, and success — the same ones Nouwen explained that confronted Jesus in the desert. I saw in myself the obvious signs that I was still far away from home: fear, sometimes terror, control, busyness, pushing myself beyond my limits as a means of gaining someone else's approval — all the extravagances of wasted energy. I too had spent just about everything I had. I began to listen for God calling me to let go, to come home, and to become more responsive in trusting him.

My journey home involved prayer and immersion into my Catholic faith, a faith I had come to take for granted and at times

---

*Henri Nouwen, *The Return of the Prodigal Son: A Story of Homecoming* (New York: Doubleday, 1992).

wholeheartedly dismissed. Daily Mass and regular spiritual direction became the embracing arms I would seek as I journeyed toward my place of belonging. My prayer life deepened and became the compass for my path. I saw that my full restoration would involve the experience of God's immeasurable love. I became the sinner who cast myself upon his mercy. I sought my center in the heart of an awaiting God through centering prayer, meditation upon Scripture, silent retreats, journaling, and countless books. My search for wholeness will continue for the rest of my life.

Last fall, I offered a book study group for my parish on my favorite Nouwen classic, *The Return of the Prodigal Son*. I was ready to reread the text, to reexplore my identification with each character. Any time we reread a book, different elements stir our hearts and minds, especially when we discuss the content with others, each sharing bits of our journeys that resonate with the text.

Toward the end of the study program, a conflict emerged in my life with a family member, triggering my childhood pain of not belonging, of feeling misunderstood and unwelcome. Actually, it was a major confrontation in which I was told that my behavior about something was unacceptable. My impulse was to respond as a child, to react from that old place of fear and intimidation as I always had. I was amazed by my emotional overreaction and fearful response, my knee-jerk attempt to gain approval, even as I was being hammered down. But sitting there in the midst of the heated discussion, I suddenly accessed compassion and mature love such as I had never experienced before in the presence of this loved one. I was filled with a divine energy, an incomprehensible love in the face of harsh judgments and sarcastic remarks. I had found freedom. I had also uncovered forgiveness. In those moments, I felt like I was finally growing up.

The next morning, I sat with Nouwen's book to pray the conclusion. The last section of the book, "Becoming the Father," is a call to embrace my spiritual parenthood. His words became a prayer: "The final stage of the spiritual life is to fully let go of all fear. My final vocation is indeed to become like the Father and to live out his divine compassion in my daily life." I thought of the compassion I had felt the night before and wondered again if it wasn't divine.

I read these timely words that sent a chill up my spine: "Every son and daughter has to consciously choose to step beyond their childhood and become father and mother for others. I cannot remain a child forever. I cannot keep pointing to my father as an excuse for my life. I have to dare to stretch out my own hands in blessing and to receive with ultimate compassion my children, regardless of how they feel or think of me."

I reread the stirring words: *I cannot keep pointing to my father as an excuse for my life* and considered that I must move forward with a resurrected heart. I thought of all of the *children* I was being called to love as the Father/Mother, every single loved one or friend who had been difficult to embrace. I knew it was time to let go of other people's opinions of me, that what God thinks of me is of ultimate importance and that what others think is truly irrelevant.

I read on and wept: "To become like the Father whose only authority is compassion, I have to shed countless tears and so prepare my heart to receive anyone, whatever their journey has been, and forgive them from the heart. Just as the Father gives his very self to his children, so must I give my very self to my brothers and sisters."

I could feel my Father's loving arms encircling me, offering his overflowing comfort and love to me. I knew I would never be the same. God had staked a claim on my heart. He had offered me his compassion, I was sure of that. It was a compassion I would continue to offer to others. I would soon be amazed by how much more he wanted to give me.

THE FOLLOWING SATURDAY, a mid-November day, Easton and I drove the two and a half hours to Katrina-ransacked New Orleans so I could meet with my spiritual director, Sister Gloria. In addition to my need for her wise guidance, I was anxious to view my beloved city and to ride through my old neighborhood, like a bittersweet attendance at a loved one's wake. Though I had grown up in New Orleans, after leaving for college thirty years ago, I seldom had returned, part of the reason being that my entire family had since relocated in Lafayette. But in a way, it was still home. Deep inside I knew that this excursion was to be the final leg of my trip "home."

My visit with Sister Gloria was exactly what my soul needed. She affirmed the growth that had taken place in me since our last visit months before, as well as the divine invitation to become responsible in my loving. She cautioned me to be responsible in the areas where God wants me to be, and to be more conscientious in trusting God. Sister also affirmed that Jesus had been standing with me the other day during that difficult interaction, telling me that he's confident in me. She confirmed that my homecoming was taking place, that I was indeed coming home to a strengthened relationship with God. She left me with the task of discovering "the history of Robin" as seen through no one's eyes but God's. I found that challenge intriguing and left to continue my day with Easton.

Driving across the 17th Street Canal and into a part of the city that had been heavily flooded when the levee breached, I could hardly believe the destruction. Easton drove carefully through ravaged streets, and I wiped tears as we both viewed the disaster. We drove across Pontchartrain Boulevard, past the area where debris was dumped, indeed the burial place of countless refrigerators and mammoth amounts of unrecognizable trash. The mountain of garbage stood a hundred feet high, a visible sign of an unfathomable reality.

Approaching the streets around Lakeview, the area of New Orleans where I grew up, I noticed the tattered sign for French Street and asked Easton to take a right. The home of my childhood friends, the Vogt family, was in that first block on French Street and I wanted to see it.

Stepping outside the car, my heart sank. The home in front of me was destroyed, the loving homestead where Mr. Charlie and Mrs. Lena and their four children had lived. "Miss Lena," as we called her, was my mother's best friend, an Elizabeth to Mamma and even to me, especially during the years after Daddy's death when I had sought comfort with her loving family. I had spent much of my childhood at this home of belonging and had loved it there.

Glancing at the water lines left by the floodwaters, like ribbons of dirt encircling the front columns and wound tightly around the entire façade, I felt a jolt of disbelief. Those dark lines seemed to be holding the shattered house together. My eyes scanned the pink fluorescent markings made by the rescue workers, the broken porch swing, and the dead, debris-covered lawn. I remembered the goodness here and imagined scenes from long ago that had taken place behind those now blemished walls — countless hours playing with the three girls while our moms were nourished at the kitchen table by warm coffee and one another's presence. I could almost taste the homemade biscuits that had nurtured my soul, prepared with love by Miss Lena's mother, Maw Maw Schillesci, and I longed to hear Maw Maw traipsing across the terrazzo floors once again in her fuzzy rubber-soled slippers on her way to the kitchen. I imagined the scent of Jungle Gardenia perfume, which JoAnn, Vicki, and I would occasionally sneak from their older sister, Lynet. I remembered the hot tea that Miss Lena had prepared for me with love one day when I wasn't feeling well. During my tough adolescence, I had breathed in the life of that family and the tender love they had offered, a love that no storm could obliterate.

Remaining motionless amid the terrible destruction, I glanced down at the muddy street and glimpsed an object, unidentifiable and obviously ruined by the floodwaters. Curious, I stooped down to see what it was and carefully opened the cover. I had come across a photo album, the plastic pages dingy from the ordeal, the photographs water-stained and mostly unrecognizable. I turned over the first page, slowly making out the faded picture of Vicki as a young schoolgirl. I was stunned that I had discovered one of their family treasures and felt warmly connected to all of them, but saddened even more by their loss. I turned another page and recognized a childhood picture of me! How loved I felt in that moment, belonging to this precious family. I carefully turned over more pages only to discover another picture of me, taken on a day when the girls and I had dressed up their cat. Turning again, I spotted another photograph taken when I was somewhat older, tenderly holding my brand-new godchild. It was mind-boggling to consider my place in this family, to know that Miss Lena had posted my pictures along with her own children's. It struck me deeply that I found the album on that particular day, over ten weeks after the storm, having worked so hard in recent weeks to return to my divine home. God clearly wanted me to see in that photo album an image of the loved, authentic child that I truly was. God was indeed kissing me and welcoming me back home, revealing his "history of Robin" right there in that album. I felt overwhelmed by his goodness, by the kindness offered me throughout my life. I owned my daughtership that day, the lavish comfort of belonging.

Carefully folding up the album, I gently placed it in our trunk, knowing I would get it back to the family, but aware that the find was a testimony for my own soul, serendipitously placed there for me as a healing. (I would discover later that of the few pictures that had survived, perhaps about twenty of a few hundred, most of them were of me, spanned across the years of my youth.) I took great joy in having several pictures of the Vogt family restored, and I recently returned them all to a grateful, loving Miss Lena and Mr. Charlie.

The next evening, my Theresian sisters and our husbands gathered for our annual Thanksgiving Mass in my home. During the Mass I glanced around at the faces of these wonderful people I loved, in many ways a family. We sang together and celebrated the Eucharist beneath the famous Rembrandt painting of *The Return of the Prodigal Son* that hangs over my mantle. The painting had been a wedding present from my siblings to Easton and me, truly one of the most touching gifts of my life, incredibly thoughtful and in many ways a generous gift of peace. Listening to the singing voices, I smiled inside and reflected on the gathering, for me a deeply personal celebration of my homecoming. Looking up at the painting, I felt the comfort of the one who had returned to claim her place and thanked God for loving me so deeply, for carving me on the palm of his hand. Our fatted calf that evening was the delicious Thanksgiving feast cooked with love by each of us. What a celebration it was!

PRODIGAL ONE, thank you for showing me that I, too, had scattered the riches that our Father gave me and had recklessly forgotten his glory. And thank you for remembering your divine inheritance so that I could remember mine. You showed me the way home, right into the arms of a Father who loves us both with an everlasting love. May we never forget to celebrate our moments of homecoming and to live assured that we are always at home, cared for by a Love beyond our wildest dreams.

— R.H.

# 10

# *The Baker Woman*

## *I Bring Bread to the World*

He told them another parable. "The kingdom of heaven is like leaven
which a woman took and hid in three measures of flour, till it was
all leavened."
— Matthew 13:33

Jesus teaches that everyday life is the place of the sacred. The temple
is no longer the place to look for it. Everyday life is the arena where
the kingdom is the most powerful.
— Father Thomas Keating, *The Parables of Jesus*

So we have another instance of Jesus's depicting divine nature in
female terms. In first-century culture, had Jesus done that only once,
that one instance would have been extraordinary. The fact that he
did it repeatedly strongly drives home the point of human equality.
— Virginia Ramey Mollenkott, *The Divine Feminine*

> Father,
> We are all hungry baby birds this morning.
> Our heart-mouths are gaping wide,
> Waiting for you to fill us.
> — *God Is No Stranger:*
> *A Haitian Prayer Book from Light Messages*

 In the famous passage above from Matthew's Gospel, Jesus tells us that the kingdom of God is like a woman who adds yeast to flour and makes bread. This earthy image is not surprising, coming from the Lord Jesus, a man who spoke of God in fields of grain, lost coins and sheep, and virgins at a wedding. As I meditated with this Gospel passage, I decided to enter into a living reflection of the parable by making bread and seeing what insights I might gain as I baked. I decided this with some trepidation because I have had some disasters in trying to bake bread, but in the service of this book, I decided to try once again.

I looked at a number of recipes and combined some desired features from several that looked promising. I typed up my new recipe and printed it on pretty blue cardstock. On the morning of my baking prayer, I wrote the Matthew scripture in red on a three-by-five card and propped it on my counter. Then I gathered rusty-brown sunflowers from my garden, placed them in a blue aluminum coffeepot, and set them nearby. I lit a candle on my baking altar, and then I got out a large wooden bowl, held it up high, and said a prayer, "God of the universe, bless the work of my hands, the work of my hands."

The first step of the bread-making process was to dissolve yeast in warm water. If the yeast wasn't good, the whole project would be a flop. I microwaved some water and stirred in the yeast.

*Is this the way it is with your kingdom, Dear One; our yeast must be alive? If our yeasty spirits are dead, then we can't spread your joy, your good news. If the material cares of the world take away all of our yeastiness, then the bread of life becomes flat, hardly edible. But you are the one who can take our little and multiply it. Let my yeast be good, Lord, strong enough to grow, and bubble, and bake up so sweet — bread for the kingdom.*

I felt the ancient Baker Woman of the Gospel beside me as I began to melt butter and measure sugar, salt, and flour, glancing at the yeast in the water and wondering whether it should be fizzing or something to indicate its aliveness. I thought about how all the ingredients in the bread rely upon the yeast to come into fullness, bringing the power of Jesus's parable to mind. As I mixed the good, basic foodstuffs in my bread bowl, I felt connected to all the women across the world, across the centuries, who have made bread for their families. They used bowls like mine, and flour drifted over their counters like snow. They knew that making the stuff of life was often messy and uncertain. They prayed that their yeast was good and their butter was sweet. As I bake, I am connected to all who say, "Give us this day our daily bread."

*God, so present here in my kitchen, gather with me at my kitchen altar. I see all the different ingredients that are needed in this bread and know that if any one was left out, it would be greatly missed. That is the way you feel about your kingdom, isn't it? You want all of us, all the parts of us, and all the kinds of us across this world. None are better, none more needed than the others. If only we could see this and stop our fighting over who is right and who has the truth. Then we could feed the bread of life to each other.*

I scoop the moist dough out onto the counter and visualize the baking woman of the parable, so brown and knowing with a twinkling smile. God is the bread-bearer in our world, and God kneads us and shapes us. Now I work the dough beneath my hands — this is the best part! Flour on the bread board, flour on my hands, the dough so springy and filled with life, soft and cool, brown with whole wheat flour. Just as I am connected to all those who make food, I am connected to God who brings to us any abundance we have, and I give thanks for strong hands, a secure home, and for all that I have to eat and to wear. The woman who baked the bread so long ago did not bake for fun, as I am doing, but in order to sustain life. I think of all those around the world who must toil daily just to eat. I want to be more grateful for all that I have.

*Thank you, God, for food, without which we could not live. We say with the psalmist: "The hand of the Lord feeds us, God answers all our needs." Let us not take food for granted as we remember those who have so little. May we honor the work done with hands, the simple work of the world done by so many.*

I put the kneaded bread mixture back into its bread bowl, and now the moment of truth comes. Will the dough rise; will it double in size as promised? Will the yeast do its work? I butter the top of the dough and place it on the open and warmed oven door. Now I must wait.

*Holy Spirit, if I try to force myself to rise artificially, I will destroy what you are creating in me. Teach me patience, knowing that your kingdom will come each day if I put down my agenda, and open my eyes, and just do what I am called to do, as the woman in the parable did. Make me bread well-kneaded by your loving hands.*

The dough rises, and I look at it fondly, this work of my hands. God looks upon us, God's creations, like this, I think. God looks with fondness, waiting to see what we shall become.

My bread dough is nut brown and moist, rich with butter and eggs. I turn it onto the floured bread board once again and knead it a few times, breaking it apart and putting it into three little bread pans. I reflect as I break the bread apart:

Jesus is bread broken on the altar of our churches as life for the world. As we imitate him, our spirits can be bread that is broken when we feel others' pain and extend ourselves to meet the needs of many. We can be sustenance for the weary and discriminated-against when we stand up against the injustices they face, knowing that people may misunderstand. Sometimes our hearts are broken like this bread when we try to ease the pain of our friends, children, and others in our lives. Give us strength.

*We want to be like you, our God of the little things, our God of the bigger things, the Woman who bakes the bread, and then becomes the bread she bakes.*

The loaves rise one more time, and then I slide them into the hot oven. Soon the house is filled with the nutty fragrance of baking bread. My husband, Dee, comes in for lunch and we share a warm slice with yogurt spread that melts on our fingers. The bread is delicious, really good! I am almost surprised because I have tried to bake homemade bread before with much less success. Perhaps this bread is better because it is soaked with prayer. I pour some cold milk into a glass and take time to savor my simple meal. "Give me this day my daily bread," I think. I wrap up the other two loaves to give to friends while they are still fresh.

*Thank you, Spirit, for the yeast doing its work.*

*Thank you, Jesus, for elevating the simple and wonderful things that fill our days to the altar of the holy.*

*You understood about yeast, and bread, and hunger, and cooking for the kingdom.*

*Jesus, you spoke of God as the Good Shepherd, and God as the Baker Woman, images that still resonate deeply within us. You brought God close to the simple tasks that men and women must do each day.*

*You understood women, and we love you for it. May we shine in your kingdom, may we dance around your table.*

*Amen.*

## Baker Woman Bread

Assemble ingredients and utensils. I used three measuring cups, but you might do better! You need a big bowl; if you have a big wooden one, it adds an authentic touch. And, if the Spirit moves you, don't forget to add a special ingredient — prayer!

### Ingredients

2 packages yeast
1/2 cup warm, not hot, water
1/2 cup sugar
1 teaspoon salt
3/4 cup warm, whole milk
4 cups white flour
1 cup whole wheat flour
1 stick real, salted butter (not light) melted and cooled some
4 tablespoons corn oil
2 eggs, lightly beaten

## *Instructions*

Stir the yeast into the warm water and let it set for five minutes. In another bowl, mix together the sugar and salt, then pour in the milk and stir well. Beat in one cup of the white flour, the butter and corn oil, the eggs, and the yeast mixture. When well blended, add the rest of the flour (three cups of white and one of whole wheat) and mix with your hands thoroughly. Turn the dough out onto a floured bread board and then knead, turning it about eight or so times, until dough is smooth.

Place the dough back in the bread bowl, and oil the top of the dough with a little melted butter or corn oil. Cover the bowl loosely and place it in a warm, draft-free place to rise. Let the dough rise for about ninety minutes, until doubled.

Place the dough on a bread board and knead it several times. Divide the dough into three equal pieces, and place them in small oiled loaf pans — four and one-half inches by eight and one-half inches — or make rolls. Let the dough rise for thirty or so minutes. Bake at 375° for about fifteen minutes for rolls and thirty minutes for loaves.

This bread is really good and not difficult to make. It is not a historically accurate recipe from biblical times, but one that tested well for me. Make it with a friend and share it fresh out of the oven with coffee! It is best eaten in a couple of days as it does not contain preservatives. My husband, Dee, likes it best baked into rolls. —L.H.D.

# 11

# The Hemorrhaging Woman

## We Have but Touched Your Hem

Now there was a woman who had been suffering from hemorrhages for twelve years. She had endured much under many physicians, and had spent all that she had; and she was no better, but rather grew worse. She had heard about Jesus, and came up behind him in the crowd and touched his cloak, for she said, "If I but touch his clothes, I will be made well." Immediately her hemorrhage stopped; and she felt in her body that she was healed of her disease. Immediately aware that power had gone forth from him, Jesus turned about in the crowd and said, "Who touched my clothes?" And his disciples said to him, "You see the crowd pressing in on you; how can you say, 'Who touched me?'" He looked all around to see who had done it. But the woman, knowing what had happened to her, came in fear and trembling, fell down before him, and told him the whole truth. He said to her, "Daughter, your faith has made you well; go in peace, and be healed of your disease."          — Mark 5:25–34

What do you tell them,
across the ages, sister?
Whisper to me, sister,
what was it
that happened to you?
When did life stir in you again?
Was it a voice you heard or
a dream you dreamt?

...Tell me, sister, tell me—
that I might whisper your story
and your secret
to your sisters imprisoned
across the globe!

— Edwina Gately, *Soul Sisters*

One might say that when [the woman] touched the hem of Jesus's garment she was *essentially* healed and when she spoke with Jesus explicitly and told him the whole truth she was *fully* healed. Simply put, what [the text] tells us is that, just like this woman, we will find healing and wholeness by touching the Body of Christ and, as members of the Body of Christ, we are called upon to dispense God's healing and wholeness by touching others.

— Ronald Rolheiser, *The Holy Longing*

I think I like the narrative of the hemorrhaging woman best of all the stories of women in the Bible. Hers is a remarkable story of transformation — the result of one gallant movement of the woman's hand to touch a garment, though not just any garment. She had stood alone in the midst of a jeering crowd with one tiny thread of hope in her heart. In the center of her being, she somehow knew that if she could but touch a tiny part of his clothing she would be healed of a dozen years of bleeding and perhaps a lifetime of fear, poverty, isolation, and despair. The unnamed woman risked, reaching inward for courage and outward for the hem of transforming love, and her life was never the same. I have experienced the privilege of reaching for that same hem. I have also had the pleasure of witnessing others reach long and hard for it.

The hemorrhaging woman's story came alive for me when I participated in a sort of communal hem touch in an isolated village in northeast Mexico with some destitute women, who like the heroine in the story, exist in broken, hopeless, and shattered lives. I'm not sure which part I played in that holy scene. All I know is that since then, my life has not been the same either.

The women had migrated together to a desolate site beside a Mexican highway in search of a way to make a living. They began an industry that started out as a cantina and ended up offering occasional pleasure to passing truck drivers. They had little choice in how to make ends meet and were doing the best they could. Perhaps the first holy hem they ever touched was that of missionaries from Family Missions Company, Catholic lay missionary-evangelists, based in our area. The missionaries fell in love with the women and their children, moved by their isolation and the stigma of their situation, for they had been shunned, even by most Catholic clergy. They worked for several years to help heal the women's collective hemorrhages of loneliness and despair.

I discovered those beautiful souls almost by accident, when my Theresian sister Tish innocently asked me one day just before our annual mission trip if we might use a sewing machine, one she was willing to donate for our missionary efforts. I simply didn't know — a sewing machine was not something we'd ever brought to the poor whom we serve, but her innocent question led me to find out about the women, living in a village called Kilometer 64, and a project that I would wrap my heart around instantly.

It turned out that there was a small fund to help the women initiate a cottage industry, which would enable them to learn to sew and sell children's clothes, hopefully to make enough money that they could forego their present degrading business efforts. Nothing much had happened with the project with the exception of a multitude of prayers. But people are amazingly generous. When our mission vans pulled out of Lafayette, Louisiana, just over a week later, we were loaded down with a dozen sewing machines, incredible quantities of fabric and sewing notions, spools of thread donated by every student from an area Catholic school, and enough cash to get our project under way. Our hearts were as packed full as those trailers, overflowing with the love and prayers and generosity that had poured forth from our community. We were on our way to Kilometer 64 to provide hems, lots of hems.

AS I ARRIVED AT THE VILLAGE on a Monday morning, the questions that had loomed the previous week stood before me: Would the women be open to our missionary efforts? Would they welcome our aid to offer them a greater sense of dignity, and would they in fact want this new business venture? My mind had conjured many images of what their village would look like and how welcoming the women would be. As we drove up to the property, I felt taken aback by the desolation, a barrenness I would quickly discover that existed only in the surroundings and not at all in the hearts of the people.

Dotting their desert property were about a dozen dilapidated buildings, a windmill-driven water well, and sparse vegetation. I couldn't help but wonder where the residents lived. I figured out quickly that the tiny adobe building toward the back of the desert acreage would be our work site. I had been told that finishing the structure would be our major work project for the week, as it would eventually serve the dual purpose of chapel and sewing room. I would need the patience of the hemorrhaging woman, the patience that poor abandoned outcast women must develop, to forego my Americanized business plan to have the women sewing by the week's end. There wasn't even electricity in their village to run a sewing machine.

No sooner had our van pulled to a stop than we were warmly greeted and welcomed by three of the women residents, middle-aged women like myself. Looking back on that moment now, I can sense that the embodiment of the hemorrhaging woman was standing before me. Present in their spirits were stark vulnerability and visible brokenness. Yet there was an unmistakably strong resolve in their eyes, deep penetrating eyes that revealed determination and a longing to connect. The woman's eyes that looked upon Jesus that day as he passed on that crowded street must have had that same intensity. Despite the harsh lifestyle in the village of Kilometer 64, the women had a spark intact, a light I recognized within myself, perhaps the only feature we had in common. Using my limited Spanish vocabulary I asked their names, and within moments a sisterhood began to unfold.

Julia, Sofia, and Isabel — our greeters that first morning — and other women gathered each day to lend a hand spreading the robin's egg blue color on the concrete walls of the small building. The village elder, Tomasa, had striking gray hair, swept back to reveal a weathered face — the kind you see in *National Geographic* — marked with the scars of hardship and suffering, and the tenderness of age and wisdom. With arms always folded, a sign of her meekness, she would entrust her quiet, calming presence to our workplace each day. Teenage girls, beautiful young women, often with high heels on their feet and babies on their hips, brought freshness and eagerness to the site. We all took turns holding babies, playing Duck Duck Goose with toddlers and adolescents, and painting the walls. We were becoming a little community with one goal in mind: hope.

When some of the men took over preparing the dirt floors for cement, we took time to visit the women in their homes. One day, I brought bread that had been donated by our friend Josephina, who owns a nearby restaurant where we stopped on our way to the village from the town where we stay. She handed us several loaves of freshly baked bread when she found out where we were headed. When Isabel received her loaf, she explained that she had already had her bread that day and would pass the loaf on to the others. I knew I would never again pray "Give us this day our daily bread" without the sting of that memory in my heart and a call to be more generous.

When I heard Tomasa apologize for their poverty, I felt an overwhelming sense of sadness that she felt different from us and an embarrassment that all of my privileges were so obvious. I pondered over her extreme physical poverty with an awareness that she is rich in many ways that I am poor — in courage and fortitude, perseverance and patience. I yearned for her to know that I wanted to apologize for my own poverty. How could I so easily take my life for granted?

Midweek our growing sisterhood of about twenty-five women was seated in a sacred circle on the cracked desert earth praying *Lectio Divina* with Psalm Twenty-Three. Glancing at those beautiful faces that were now becoming familiar, I felt a sense of peace, a feeling of being at home. Listening to one of our missionaries translate the heartfelt prayers of the Mexican women, their challenges seemed similar to our own. Isabel articulated their shared longing to understand Scripture and a deep desire for the continued experience of community. It occurred to me that community is not inherent, not even among women who live together. A plight the hemorrhaging woman knew well I'm sure. "Please don't forget about us" became their collective plea.

By Friday the chapel was finished and we planned a grand celebration, loading the vans with the mass of sorted clothing we had brought from the States, newly purchased Bibles, scapulars, and a carefully selected statue of Our Lady of Guadalupe acquired the day before in Saltillo — all tangible symbols of hope and remembrances of our blessed time together. We even packed a massive lunch of gorditas — yummy stuffed tacos. But mostly we brought along twenty-six missionary hearts filled with love and a supreme sense of fulfillment.

Everyone from the village turned out for that glorious morning of prayer. Entering the chapel and glimpsing the love spread across the newly painted walls, my heart flooded with joy as I read each of our names, printed carefully on taped-up newsprint thank-you notes, drawn from a list we had exchanged the previous day for prayer partnering. Along with the missionaries that had come before us, I too had fallen in love with these women, as I suspect Jesus had with the hemorrhaging woman that long ago day on a busy street.

It would take a year for our dream to be fulfilled and the sewing to commence, but soon enough, that little adobe building would become a seedbed of joy — where despair would give way to hope and creativity would birth dignity.

JUST TWO WEEKS prior to our mission trip the next year, the sewing had begun, led by local women who made the forty-five-minute trek to the village from the little town of General Cepeda to give sewing lessons. The morning of our arrival, the hum of those sewing machines and the generator outside sparked a melody in each of our hearts — a song of hope shared soul to soul. Glancing around the sewing room, I observed slight smiles on sun-scorched faces, seeds of pride gently sprouting.

Our missionaries sewed with the women all week, entertained children, folded fabric, and organized notions. I practiced my Spanish names for colors with help from the three- and four-year-old niñas eager to sort multicolored buttons. Through these basic tasks so vital to the female psyche, it was as if we were sorting all of their lives. The seamstresses worked double time each day, since we had promised to purchase whatever was ready by week's end.

There was one thing missing for me all week, however. It was my friend Isabel, the woman I'd met the year before whose spirit had since nested in my heart. "¿Dónde está Isabel?" I asked each day, inquiring about her whereabouts, only to be told every time that she had worked the night before. I figured that I'd see her at their La Levantada celebration on Wednesday night, a community-wide gathering to commemorate the official end of the Christmas season, a celebration they had put off until we could be present and share it with them. But Isabel was nowhere to be found that night either. Glancing through the dense crowd, I noticed several of the girls who hadn't been around during the day for the sewing classes, young pregnant girls. My heart sank into despair, facing the reality that nothing had changed, that probably nothing would change. In an instant, I became the hemorrhaging woman elbowing my way through the crowded judgments of my own mind. I exited the packed chapel to breathe in the night air and clear out my discouragement. Gazing up at the stars of the vast desert sky, I prayed for one healing caress to soothe my struggling heart.

In morning prayer the next day, seated among my missionary sisters and brothers, we sang our beloved mission theme song, "The Servant Song." That morning, the melody seeped into my soul as I reflectively chanted the stirring words. My mind briefly left the room; I felt lifted into a private space where Jesus and I stood alone. In the teeming street within my own heart, I reached to touch his hem and confessed my sin. I seemed to hear him whisper: "Don't you dare give in to discouragement, Robin. It is *I* that makes all things new, not *you*. I need you to be a beacon of hope only. Let me do the rest." Accompanying my tender grief was the relief of recognizing that all I ever need to do is show up. All I need to do is offer one hem of hope to another. That's what it means to be a servant, to be Jesus to another.

As we drove out to the village for our final gathering of that trip, it crossed my mind to pray with the women using the Scripture about the hemorrhaging woman. We had spent less time in prayer that week than the previous year, hoping to give them all the time they needed for their sewing. But for their efforts to ultimately make a difference, they needed to be embedded in prayer in order to entrust their work to God.

I stood before my sisters, Bible in hand, carefully reading the narrative, pausing after each verse for the Spanish translation, aware that some of the women might be hearing the story for the first time. The account of the hemorrhaging woman unfolded: There was a woman who had been suffering from hemorrhages for twelve years. She had heard about Jesus, and she came up behind him in the crowd and touched his cloak.

"If I but touch his clothes, I will be made well." Immediately her hemorrhage stopped. . . . Jesus turned about in
the crowd and said, "Who touched my clothes?" . . . The
woman . . . fell down before him, and told him the whole
truth. "Daughter, your faith has made you well; go in
peace, and be healed of your disease." (Mark 5:28–34)

As if Jesus stood before us asking the community, "Who
touched my clothes?" one by one we responded. My Theresian
sister Vicki spoke up first, exposing the agonizing pain of years
of sexual abuse. She shared her firsthand knowledge of what
it means to be used as the object of someone else's pleasure,
and her conviction that God wants us to live our lives in loving
relationships, not in relationships that make us feel less and
less about ourselves.

One of our Mexican sisters, Marilena, sitting beside Vicki
wept. They wept in one another's arms. Something Vicki had
said touched a hidden part of Marilena. Perhaps she too had
been the object of someone else's pleasure and had deep
wounds to heal.

Patty shared the ache of physical and emotional abuse by an
angry husband, a frightening time when she decided to leave,
when she actually ran away with her child to begin a new life.

Ellen, who had spent the week becoming endeared to the
children through her loving and playful attention to them, described the grief of never having borne children as an empty
space inside. We all touched into the deep sadness that Ellen
held before us. With her heart still wide open, she reflected
aloud on her gratitude for the love their children had shown

her each day. Ellen wanted their mothers to know that she had experienced God's love through their children.

Julia shared her constant worry about her ailing sister, frustrated by her helplessness at being unable to fix the illness. Marilena offered us the frustration she felt with herself over her lack of discipline, the self-control she needed to make changes in her life. A voice from the crowd assured her that she wasn't alone.

It turned out that we had lots in common, lots more than the light in their eyes evident the first time we met. The sparks in all of our eyes were now set ablaze, fanned by love, caring, concern for one another. We had each had hemorrhages, which had been soothed if not healed. And we had all been hems of transforming love. Many had fallen down before him and told the whole truth. Our faith had made us well.

I stood to conclude our prayer and to begin the difficult farewells, grasping about to offer a last message of hope. And then I saw it, the hem on a garment, a newly sewn set of yellow-checked pajamas with matching rickrack at the bottom. I held the garment before the community, like an article in a second-grade show-and-tell exercise — a visual reminder of all we had shared. I suggested that when they sew those hems they think of us, of our love for them. I prayed that they'd believe we would not forget them, believe we would pray for them, and trust that we would be back. I offered the idea that each time they sewed a hem, they consider it as the hem of Jesus and always remember that anything can be healed through touching that hem. Holding that garment in my hands, I knew that something had been healed in me that day. Like the woman in our story, I too left in peace.

OH, OUTCAST WOMAN, my heart still aches for the desperation you must have felt for far too many years. As hard as I try, I cannot imagine what you endured. But what I can envision are my own lesions and the hemorrhages of those with whom I have been privileged to journey. Thank you for showing the way, for seeking the light, for stretching far so that your story could be told and that others might know how to reach out as you did. Be assured that your story continues to stretch across the globe and that we, your sisters, are still reaching, reaching far and long. —R.H.

## Family Missions Company

Family Missions Company is a Catholic lay missionary non-profit organization. Dedicated to evangelizing the poor all over the world, they focus especially on developing countries, where they serve with zeal, love, and a commitment to the Gospel message. They were founded by Frank and Genie Summers, two natives of South Louisiana who, after experiencing a deep conversion, sold all that they had and became foreign missionaries. Frank and Genie draw upon over thirty years of missionary experience, having circumnavigated the globe with a family of seven children, to train and send out Catholic lay missionaries through FMC. Still based in Louisiana, FMC missionaries have served in places such as Mexico, Ecuador, St. Vincent and the Grenadines, Malaysia, Thailand, and the Philippines. For more information, contact *praisingcajun@yahoo.com.*

# 12

# Mary, the Mother of Christ

## Blessed Mary of the Storm

But standing by the cross of Jesus were his mother, and his mother's
sister, Mary the wife of Clopas, and Mary Magdalene.

—John 19:25b

Mary is the feminine embodiment of the divine quality of compassion.

—Joyce Rupp, *Your Sorrow Is My Sorrow*

> Compassionate One,
> I sit with empty hands
> trusting that your presence
> embraces my pain,
> shelters my vulnerability,
> and gives meaning
> to my countless dyings.
>
> —Joyce Rupp, *Your Sorrow Is My Sorrow*

 My family and I were shielded from the effects of
Hurricane Katrina. I live near Lafayette, Louisiana,
which is several hundred miles from the epicenter of that devastating hurricane. Our area was not much affected. After
flooding killed many people and devastated thousands of
homes in and around New Orleans, Hurricane Rita hit the Lake

Charles area furiously. People both west and south of me were displaced, their homes flooded during this new storm.

Because we in the Lafayette area remained relatively unaffected during both of these tragedies, our homes and public buildings became refuges for victims as thousands poured into our neighborhoods. I felt sad and helpless as I watched the aftermath of nature's fury on television and saw the many displaced families enter my town seeking sanctuary.

During this emotional time, I happened to pick up a favorite book, Joyce Rupp's *Your Sorrow Is My Sorrow*. This poignant volume takes the reader through Mary's sorrows, starting with Simon's predictions in the Temple as Mary holds the infant Jesus and ending with Christ's death upon the cross. I used this book to pray with Mary and to ponder with her about the devastation. I wondered how I could help even one of the thousands around me who were in pain and searching for a way to recover and go on with their lives.

As I entered more and more deeply into this contemplation of Mary, the mother of Christ, I embraced her fully as the Compassionate One. I saw her with her arms outstretched gracefully over the world — arms of love, healing, empathy, and compassion. This compassionate and suffering Mary of Jesus was present to me everywhere as I embarked upon small acts of mercy toward those around me who were hurting after the storms. I saw parallels between Mary's journey and the plights of those whose lives touched mine.

During the flight into Egypt to save Jesus from Herod's wrath, Mary faced the loss of her home and so much that was familiar and sustaining to her. She had to go quickly, without time to plan for the trip. The evacuees who now crowded into shelters of all kinds near my community had experienced a similar flight. They had needed to immediately leave all that was familiar in order to save their lives and the lives of their children. To help those who had suffered this trauma, I trained with a group of volunteers. We would visit with the people in a particular shelter and offer a stress debriefing, hoping to help them take a first step toward healing from the trauma.

I entered the shelter with my group on the designated morning to find about three hundred people in a refuge that appeared clean, cool, and orderly despite the dire circumstances. The first person that I saw individually was Matthew, a young man of twenty who had been working at McDonald's when he was told to go home quickly and get ready to flee the city. He and about sixteen others had left in one pickup truck, trying to find a way out of New Orleans, only to be turned back again and again because of blocked roads and general chaos. "I felt like a rat in a maze," he said. Matthew remained worried about his sister, who was still missing.

Matthew was shocked and disoriented, not knowing what to do or where to turn. I had so little to give him except a listening ear as I fought with my own feelings of despair. Yet I am glad that I was able to share part of his story, that he trusted me enough to talk about it with me. I wonder if anyone along the road to Egypt shared the story that sent Mary and Joseph on their terrifying journey from danger so long ago. Could they trust anyone? Perhaps not. And perhaps this is why I feel that Mary listens closely to each voice of pain today. As Therese of Lisieux says, speaking to Mary, "Meditating on your life in the Gospels, I dare to look at you, to draw near to you. It is not difficult for me to believe that I am your child, for I see you mortal and suffering like me."

As that day in the shelter continued, I encountered another sorrow that Mary experienced: that of losing her child for many days. It is hard for any of us mothers to visualize that Jesus was lost for *three* days! Yet in this shelter, I met a woman whose daughters were missing. Her name was Adele, and she was the matriarch of a large family; she was sweet and warm and spoke very openly.

She began to cry as she described leaving New Orleans with nothing but the clothes she wore. "I just can't believe that we are all starting all over," she said. Adele had two daughters and a son with her in the shelter, but she did not know where her other two grown daughters were. "I pray all day," she told me through her tears; "I just pray every minute that they are all right."

I know that Mary must have prayed intensely and constantly when she and Joseph realized that Jesus was lost in the big city of Jerusalem. We're insulated from the emotion of this story now because we have heard it so many times. Yet most mothers have had the experience of losing one of their children, if only for a few minutes, and have felt the deep, cold fear and the panicky feeling that something might be really wrong.

I thought of one incident in my own life when I lost my son, Jacques, for a little while. He was about eight and I thought he was at a friend's house playing, but when I checked in with that friend I found Jacques had not been there all afternoon. Dusk was falling and I didn't know where he was, and I felt panicked. He was soon found with another friend, but my suffering during that episode shaped my compassion toward Adele. Many parents across the world have lost their children in storm, war, and famine. I think that Mary's deep compassion toward them was shaped by her own suffering when she lost Jesus in the temple.

Years later, Mary was truly helpless once again when she met Jesus on the road carrying his cross. As a mother, I shy away from even envisioning such a deeply sad situation. As Jacques grew up, when he was in pain, I was in pain. If that is codependency, most of the mothers I know have this disease! In the shelter, I sat with one young mother and held her child, Jewel, on my lap; she was about two and a half.

Jewel said little, and she didn't smile as she solemnly drew squiggly lines on paper that she called, "The big water." Her brow was tightened in concentration as she drew the big water on page after page. Her mother, Sheena, sat beside her quietly. Sheena finally said, "I didn't know she knew much about the storm; I wouldn't have thought it affected her so much." As Sheena sat there pensively, I know she was holding her daughter's distress with love and that her suffering matched and exceeded that of her child.

Later that day, I met Grace, a mother of five, in the same shelter. She told me about being in her sealed apartment during Katrina with little to drink and no air-conditioning with her five little ones, two of them in diapers. Outside her door, shootings and riots were going on. Grace told me how her children cried all day, hot and thirsty until they were finally rescued. She had the smallest Bible I had ever seen; it was well marked, with pages turned down. "I like to read the Gospel of Mark," she said. I was surprised by this statement; I am not sure why. Together, we read Psalm 91: *Be with me Lord when I am in trouble.* Mary may have recited this psalm as she stood at the foot of the cross.

That day as I looked around the crowded shelter, I saw many people who may have been whispering, "Be with me Lord!" Could those of us who had escaped the storm be Christ, or be his mother to them in some small way? Every friend that I had in the Lafayette area was helping after the disasters: they had evacuees in their homes; they were working at shelters; they were raising money or taking evacuees to job interviews or doctor appointments. In truth, most of my friends were doing a lot more than I was doing, and I sometimes felt a little ashamed about this! But each of us could only do so much. How would we face our helplessness and yet still be of aid to the suffering? Be with us, Lord.

As time passed during that saddest of seasons, I realized that almost everyone that I saw in spiritual direction in my home during this time was impacted by the storms. Teachers had lost classrooms and materials, wives and mothers were feeding and housing multitudes and teetering toward exhaustion, and businesspeople were stressed about losing accounts and income. I felt more and more that instead of running from shelter to shelter, that I was called to be still and present with them, pondering with them as I felt Mary would have done. I had much to meditate upon: Why did God allow this devastation to happen? Why did the innocent suffer? What were we to make of all this destruction, and what could we say and do as Christians?

There were no easy answers, and I guess there never will be. But it became clearer to me each day that my home was to serve as a sanctuary for a few of the storm tossed, those I saw in spiritual direction. I was called to do simple tasks like sweeping my own floor, watering my own plants, and keeping my office orderly and calm. These tasks didn't make me feel very heroic, but like Mary, perhaps, I felt called to be present and to minister to those whom God put directly in my path. Hardest of all, I was called to be still, when the world was in a whirl all around me. I prayed and remained still. Mary was my model as I lived a mostly hidden life post–Katrina and Rita.

Weeks after my first shelter visit, as the recovery efforts dragged on, I helped with a "Busy People's Retreat" at Our Lady of Wisdom Church and Student Center on the University of Louisiana campus. I was the director for James, a young college student from Chalmette who had transferred to the university after his own college had been flooded. James told me how he lost his home, his church, which was a second home to him, and his college — all in one terrifying day.

James remembered his sister's wedding before the storm. "I see her so clearly, walking through our house. Her hair is black and it was so pretty against her white veil. She was so beautiful that day!" He stopped and looked pensive. "If only we could have it again: my house, our neighborhood, the tree out back I always climbed, my grandparents next door, the people across the street that were so much like family that I could go in and make a sandwich and watch T.V. there if I wanted."

I became attached to James. How I wished I could fix the situation for him! I know that Mary feels the same way, shaped as she is by suffering. Shaped into the Compassionate One. I had to accept that my own compassion lived alongside helplessness in many ways. I prayed; I did what I could. I tried to be like Mary.

As I worked with James it became apparent that he was teetering on the edge of a serious depression. We were able to get him some psychological help through Student Counseling Services on the university campus. In this way, Our Lady of Wisdom Church community was able to be Mary to James, to be the Compassionate One with her arms of mercy extended, facing the loss, holding the pain, and beginning to lay his sorrows to rest in the tomb of memory.

My mind drifts back to Claire, a homemaker and mother of four who had worked at the shelter I first visited. In the few conversations I had with Claire there, she spoke of Mary, Christ's mother, as her inspiration. She especially loved "Rosa Mystica," the mystical rose, one of the many faces of Mary, a face which is often seen crying and in distress over the sins of the world. In contrast, Claire was a vibrant and cheerful lady who helped in an easy and quiet way. She showed few signs of the ongoing and challenging problems that she encountered at the shelter as she and the other volunteers cared for hundreds of evacuees. She didn't cry when I spoke to her about the many needs of those housed there.

Yet I knew, standing in that shelter with Claire, looking across the gym floor covered with mats and blankets, garbage bags, and plastic cartons stacked with scanty possessions — with diapers and toys — and suffering people — that every woman weeps at times. Women stand in the gap, beneath the cross, and hold the pain, lifting it up for restoration and redemption. Women wait for the resurrection, not knowing exactly what they are waiting for and certainly not knowing when it will come.

But it does come. And we must not forget, either, that in Mary the Mother of Christ we have a woman who knows for sure that the resurrection will come; she knows because she experienced it. I treasure this Mary of the resurrection and I have found her everywhere, even in the chaos left by the storms.

I found her one morning when I went to a small shelter near my home for mothers and new babies. When I walked in to deliver the things I had bought, a small, very young woman was sitting on the sofa holding an adorable baby. The women volunteers in the room proceeded to pass the baby around gently, each one cooing and rocking the little thing lovingly. It seemed to me that Becka, the baby's mother, had landed in a covey of grandmothers, a nesting place of tender, feminine love. It made me smile and warmed a place deep within me. It gave me hope.

For babies are symbols of resurrection, after all: the new life that comes and will not be denied. I know that Mother Mary was there in spirit, cradling that new baby with Becka and present in the motherly compassion and hope of those women who came to help.

I see resurrection in my friend Hazel Delahoussaye (who lost her home in Hurricane Rita). She expressed these thoughts at the recent national convention for Theresians, "God never abandoned us. God came to us in all the friends who reached out, sent packages, prayed for us, and visited us. We know we are not forgotten. We found that good things can come — even out of tragedy."

I see resurrection in Harry and Shirlen, friends of ours who were rescued from their flooded home in a military boat and spent two days in an abandoned church before being able to hitch a ride to Baton Rouge and call family. They had to abandon their home in New Orleans East, a real tomb experience for them, as they lost most of their worldly goods and said good-bye to the home that they had lived in and raised their daughter, Heidi, in for over twenty years.

Harry and Shirlen's lives were touched with resurrection when they purchased an older home near Lafayette and began to renew relationships with family and old friends that they rarely saw when they lived in New Orleans. They are enjoying the slower pace of life in southwest Louisiana.

Harry, who was best man in our wedding, has reconnected with my husband, Dee. They now go on excellent adventures, like searching for the biggest blue-point crabs in every seafood shop in the village of Delcambre, or picking baskets of satsumas at the Youngsville Fruit Farm. Dee and Harry's enjoyment of their renewed friendship has lifted my spirits also, and helped me to see the blessings that have emerged from the wreckage of the storms.

All around my beleaguered state of Louisiana, saws and hammers, and parishioners in newly painted churches now sing the song of resurrection. We are a people who will not stay down. We are a people of faith and of new beginnings. We have been shaped now, like Mary, with a compassion that will never leave us. We are changed as we look toward a new beginning, a resurrection.

We are not forgotten; we will learn to live a resurrected life. For resurrection does come; it comes after the darkest of nights; it arrives in a hundred ways, bit by bit, breath by breath. It comes when we hold on in faith and take the next step of a new life. It graces our hearts when we consider Mary, who never lost hope. Because of her hope, Mary of suffering and compassion becomes Mary of the Resurrection for us. She is the believer who first lifted her head to the Risen One and let her sorrow go. And I believe she was the first to hear Jesus say, as he stood in his new and glorious body, "Do not be afraid!" (Matthew 28:10a).　　　　　　　　　　　　　　　　　—L.H.D.

# 13

# The Woman Who Found the Lost Coin

## Rejoice with Me!

Or what woman having ten silver coins, if she loses one of them, does not light a lamp, sweep the house, and search carefully until she finds it? When she has found it, she calls together her friends and neighbors, saying, "Rejoice with me, for I have found the coin that I had lost." Just so, I tell you, there is joy in the presence of the angels of God over one sinner who repents.  —Luke 15:8–10

The world is fairly studded and strewn with pennies cast broadside from a generous hand. But — and this is the point — who gets excited by a mere penny? It is dire poverty indeed when a man is so malnourished and fatigued that he won't stoop down to pick up a penny. But if you cultivate a healthy poverty and simplicity, so that finding a penny will literally make your day, then, since the world is in fact planted with pennies, you have with your poverty bought a lifetime of days.  — Annie Dillard, *Pilgrim at Tinker Creek*

RH  There is a story in Scripture that, to me, is hardly noteworthy. The brief narrative appears sandwiched between two well-known parables, the Lost Sheep and the Prodigal Son, and obviously contains the same theme as the other more famous stories: Jesus searching for the lost ones. The heroine in the seemingly unremarkable tale is someone we know nothing about, only that she lights a lamp, sweeps her house, searches meticulously for her lost coin, and then rejoices when she finds it. I could never understand the connection between an inanimate object such as a coin and living, breathing beings like sheep and sons.

I must admit, however, that I like the spirit of this searching woman. I am drawn to her persistence and determination to find her keepsake. She obviously knows what she wants and knows what to do first in order to get it — shed the light of wisdom and careful discernment on the area she is exploring. But still, why would a woman rummaging for one lost coin be compared to Jesus searching for his lost sheep?

I discovered an appealing, even romantic explanation of her plight in William Barclay's Bible Study Series on the Gospel of Luke, which helped me grapple with her dilemma: "The mark of a married woman was a headdress made of ten silver coins linked together by a silver chain. For years maybe a girl would scrape and save to amass her ten coins, for the headdress was almost the equivalent of her wedding ring."* The possibility that the woman's search was for one missing coin of the ten that adorned her headdress — similar to a hunt for a lost wedding ring — had great appeal to me. I liked the value she placed upon being married and could better comprehend her determination to find her coin.

I, too, found a lost coin one day, someone's tossed-aside penny in the middle of the street. I wasn't looking for it, though — the penny sort of found me. But that one coin began

---

*William Barclay, *The Gospel of Luke*, rev. ed., Daily Study Bible Series (Philadelphia: Westminster Press, 1975).

a search for clarity and grace and in time for the coins for my own headdress.

I found the penny one morning as I was strolling on my daily walk. I had been praying about an issue in my life that for months had been absorbing most of my prayer and mental energy when I noticed a penny and stooped to pick it up. It seemed to bear a message. As I placed the penny in my pocket, I prayed that this simple copper coin would become a symbol of the outcome I wanted in the relationship I'd been praying about — that the relationship would unfold gently and fruitfully. A silly deal I worked out with God.

The relationship I had been prayerfully discerning had been a delightful surprise in my life, a life I'd grown comfortable living singly for quite a while. Divorced for eight years, I had developed an aptitude for making my own decisions and planning my life on its own independent terms. I had just moved into my own little home on Memory Lane and life seemed set. And then Easton came along.

A good and stable man with a passion for spirituality, he had been recently widowed. Actually I had been friends with both him and his deceased wife and had always admired their marriage. After Paula's death to cancer, Easton and I developed a special friendship. I spent a lot of time listening to his stories of their beautiful life together and helping him bear his grief. In many ways it was nice to have a newfound friend, to enjoy time with a male companion, even a grieving one. There was a depth in his spirit that was attractive, and I felt at ease in his presence. Soon enough, though, much too soon for either of us, my heart began to wrap around his. My head knew better, but my heart was leading the way. I had never imagined having such a special man in my life, one I could talk with so freely and with whom I could enjoy so many common interests. I was finding myself becoming attached quickly, an issue I had struggled with most of my life. On my walk the morning I found the coin, I was praying as I had done so often to slow my heart down and proceed with caution. I knew he wasn't ready to love again, and in fact just needed a good friend. I had to keep reminding myself of that fact and to remain in prayer.

That evening Easton and I went out for coffee. As we approached the coffeehouse, I noticed a man reach down on the ground and pick up something, then toss it toward Easton and me. The tiny object that landed at our feet was a penny. I was stunned by the synchronicity and wondered whether it, in fact, had been tossed by a generous Hand. What could this innocent but strange gesture mean?

Like the woman in our story, I was about to become a searcher, determined to seek and find lost coins — the coins of trust, discernment, surrender, and healthy detachment. What I didn't realize at the time was that God was searching for me. I was the coin about to be found.

Over the many months that followed our evening at the coffee shop, and as Easton and I grew fonder of one another, I found pennies in the strangest locations. Their discovery always seemed timed perfectly: there was the penny I found in my bed in General Cepeda, Mexico, on the mission trip I embarked upon the day Easton decided he needed some "space" in our relationship. That's when a fellow missionary offered me the Annie Dillard quote that I used as an epigraph to this essay. I found a penny in the drain of the drinking fountain in our student center where I work, pennies in my dryer, in parking lots, and many on the street, always discovered when my vulnerable heart needed reassurance. There was also the penny glued to a magnet that was attached to a friend's refrigerator that caught my eye just as I was sharing with her my struggle to remain detached. That penny now hangs on my own refrigerator.

My favorite penny find occurred one evening as I descended the stairway at my office on my way to visit Easton after work. We had just been through a month-long hiatus, and he had called me to come by after work for a visit, missing our friendship. I had asked God for a penny for reassurance that all would go well with our time together and then quickly realizing that my little penny game had become superstitious, prayed instantly that I would surrender this silly relationship fixation and trust in God's providence regarding my future. There was a penny on the carpeted floor at the bottom of the stairs.

Throughout my treasure hunt, a struggle remained: even though Easton and I were obviously fond of one another and growing in love, I wanted to control how the love would be lived out. I wanted to know the ending of the story, whether we would eventually be married or whether this would just turn out to be a blessed friendship. Challenging questions emerged: Was I worthy of such a life-giving love? Could I trust God with my future? Did I even want to? Telling God what I wanted had always been the easier thing to do. To sit back and listen to his plans for me had been uncharted territory.

Over time, I began to realize that there was a self I was longing to find — the part of me that could love with open hands. My search for the lost coin became a search for the woman within who was free to love without grasping, the woman who could trust God completely with her life, a God who wanted her to be happy.

One day I received a helpful message in the form of an e-mail from my daughter Emily, who had no idea of my preoccupation or my symbol, only that she and I had shared a penny connection many years before. The electronic message entitled "The Penny" carried the reminder that every U.S. coin bears the message *In God We Trust*. The story in the e-mail concerned a wealthy businessman who picks up pennies because he believes that God is dropping a message right in front of him. The man admitted: "Who am I to pass it by? When I see a coin, I pray, I stop to see if my trust IS in God at that moment. I pick the coin up as a response to God — that I do trust in Him" (author unknown).

In prayer one morning, like the woman sweeping her house while searching for her coin, I begged God to sweep my heart clean of my own desires and fill me with that trust in him. My prayer was hardly spoken when I received a striking image: my heart, spotless like a fresh blank canvas. It appeared as if, in an instant, God had taken away all of my desires. That morning, I became the treasure that God found — humble, meek, desiring nothing but to follow God's will — worthy all along of God's and another person's love. I came out of the experience with my headdress refurbished, my sense of oneness with my own soul restored. I was free.

Over the many months that followed, my trust grew, but not because of pennies. I began to see God's hand in my life, guiding and gracing me with the gift of surrender. My prayer life took on a deeper intensity accompanied by a growing awareness of God's love for me. A sense of equilibrium began to take shape within my soul as I let go of my inordinate attachment to my relationship with Easton and became passionately attached to God. Mostly, I grew in responsiveness to the power of grace as the grace of trust that I begged for daily seemed to pour down like the pennies that continued to show up on my path. Every coin seemed to represent a part of myself that God continued to heal. Each discovery appeared to bring a little more strength, a bit more courage, a lot more trust, and the deep consolation that accompanies the acceptance of God's direction in our lives.

As Easton and I both continued to prayerfully discern our future, considering carefully the effects of our relationship on our grown — and growing — children, peace grew in both of our hearts and a desire to spend our lives together took root. We were married a year and a half after the discovery of that first lost coin, a blessed time of great rejoicing and new beginnings.

The penny appearances have continued to this day, found mostly in pockets and parking lots and along streets where I might walk. Just the other day my four-year-old grandson, Hayes, proudly walked in my back door and innocently handed me a penny he'd just found. There are now sixty-eight pennies (and a few nickels and dimes) in a little yellow bank on my desk in the kitchen, some shiny new, others so tarnished they are hardly recognizable. The bank is nearly filled to the brim, as is my heart every time I find another coin and place it along with the others.

In a homily at Mass recently, the priest suggested that we ask God for signs of His love and mercy. That's exactly what the penny finds have come to mean to me — little kisses of love and mercy from a Presence that enfolds me at all times, prompting me to trust that Presence with all of my desires, desires I am learning to hold in wide-open hands. I find that when my heart is swept clean and the lamp of openness is lit, I find those little love notes from God much more readily. Whenever I come across a penny, I celebrate with my friend in Scripture who found her lost coin: "Rejoice with us! For we have found our lost coins, found the treasure of our trust in God's love and care, found a oneness with soul we had somehow lost along the way."

SEEKER OF LOST COINS, thank you for teaching me that even a penny is a gift from God and that a healthy inner poverty and surrender are great magnets for God's love and mercy. Continue to remind me often of my need to let go and to celebrate joyfully when I rediscover God's mercy, especially when I find myself grasping and demanding what I think I most need along the journey.                                                    —R.H.

# 14

# The Samaritan Woman

## I Will Give You a Drink

There came a woman of Samaria to draw water. Jesus said to her,
"Give me a drink." —John 4:7

God approaches gently, often secretly, always in love, never through
violence and fear. He comes to us, as God has told us, in those whom
we know in our own lives. Very often we do not recognize God. God
comes in many people we do not like, in all who need what we can
give, in all who have something to give us.
— Caryll Houselander, *A Child in Winter*

**LHD** It is cool enough this morning to sit on my shaded
patio beside the fountain, a perfect place to sit
and think about the Samaritan woman, that famous first
apostle whom Jesus transformed beside Jacob's well so many
years ago.

I have gathered the stuff I will use for my prayer time this
day: my Bible, my new journal with its big, unlined white pages,
a basket full of nice, new crayons, and my Tina jug. I must
begin this reflection on the Samaritan woman by telling you
about the small pottery vessel that has been broken and glued
back together, leaving the cracks and dents clearly visible. I
have had my Tina jug, a little clay-colored water pitcher, for
months — since a friend of mine, Tina, dropped it and pieced

it back together. This happened just before a retreat I was presenting on (of course) the Samaritan woman. This vessel serves as a reminder of the story and the brokenness the Samaritan woman suffered as she married many husbands and lived a chaotic life. And it is a reminder that still, despite the unworthiness she felt, Jesus chose her. The Samaritan woman is a symbol of the wounded healer, an unlikely bringer of the waters of life to others.

Now sitting here in the cool sun I gaze deeply into the fountain and see my two goldfish slipping about together, like shadows of one another in the dark blue water. There is life deep within me, too. I can feel it, and my imagination stirs as I further consider the Samaritan woman. For the first time in quite a while, I feel deeply at peace and fully ready to settle into meditation. I begin to read her story in my Bible.

Suddenly, my husband pulls up in his truck, "Turn on the hose; where's the end of it? Help me! I've got to meet someone!" He is struggling with the hose in exasperation and commenting on the fact that I don't need such a long hose. I turn on the faucet to get the water flowing, and he fills his big thermos and roars off. I am deeply aggravated, my peaceful morning disturbed; then the meaning hits me and I start chuckling. There it is — another water vessel to be filled just like that of the Samaritan woman. The need we all have for water, the fact that we all need help. I am already surrounded by messages today.

I take some centering breaths and quiet myself again. I re-open my Bible and read the texts that surround John, Chapter Four, and I see now a unity that escaped me when I had read these passages in the past. In John, Chapter Two, at Mary's urging, Jesus turns the water at a wedding into wine, his first miracle. Here is a clear message that Jesus has come to turn the water of everyday people into wine; he will make all things new and birth a lively new spirit. In John, Chapter Three, a Pharisee named Nicodemus visits Jesus in the dark of night to inquire about being born again. He insists on clinging to a literal meaning of Jesus's words (as the Samaritan woman does later on). Nicodemus asks how one can be birthed from his mother's womb. Jesus says, "The wind blows wherever it pleases and you hear the sound of it, but you cannot tell from where it comes or where it is going."

I pause in reading these words and look toward my fountain where a large bumblebee is landing heavily on the pink sage nearby. "It is in the Spirit that we are born again," I think. After this incident with Nicodemus, Jesus has his disciples go out baptizing with water. Water. Its image drenches the pages of John's Gospel, and it frames Jesus's encounter with the Samaritan woman. It is the water of Spirit. I try to descend deeply into what it all means.

Now I write Jesus's first words to the Samaritan woman in my journal in blue crayon, "Will you give me a drink?"

In my mind's eye I see the Samaritan woman: proud and even haughty, hardened by years of rejection, her silent pride hiding the scars from the years of pain she has suffered. She is the broken vessel, the jug that can barely hold water, like the Tina jug on my table. This woman's scars might have been hidden from others, but to Jesus they were clearly visible. It was unlikely that this woman would ask anyone for anything. Jesus disarms her by asking *her* for something. He catches her by surprise, genius of human nature that he is.

I am immersed deeply in my meditation now, and it seems as if Jesus and the Samaritan woman are standing beside my fountain, in Maurice, Louisiana, on a mid-July day. Jesus is standing beside her, turned toward her, his arms outstretched, his palms turned up. She is holding the battered water jar that she has been carrying around for years. As I gaze at this inner vision, I realize that Jesus has come to the Samaritan woman to turn her water into wine, to heal her pain and to baptize her into the new life that she so longs for. In order to do this, he has breached the walls of her invulnerability by asking *her* for help. As he did as a child in the manger, he has come in the guise of the helpless and needy one. "Will you give me a drink?" he asks.

This reminds me that I encountered Jesus in the guise of a helpless and needy person in my own home a few months before. My strong, faithful husband, who has always been so good at taking care of *me*, had to have a total hip replacement. It was hard for him to admit his neediness and vulnerability about the operation, but the fact was he was really going to need my help. I went to training classes at Our Lady of the Lake Hospital in order to be his caregiver. There was a lot to remember, and I was frightened. What if he fell? (I'm not that strong.) What if I couldn't move him from one place to another? What if I forgot to do something and he had complications because of me? I prayed daily during this time (Okay. I admit it, I *worried* a lot during this time) and hoped that I would rise to the occasion.

After the surgery, everything went amazingly well, and we grew closer as I did Dee's exercises with him and helped him with every aspect of daily living. I was startled to see the depths of my selfishness and impatience as the sharp edges of the battered, cracked Tina jug within me made themselves known. I had many impatient thoughts. (I just brought you some water! Are you *still* having trouble doing that?) But even these not-so-charitable thoughts, when surrendered to Spirit, deepened the worth of the experience and broadened my humility. I would like to say that Dee showered me with praise and gratitude, but that is not his way. It was enough to receive his tender kisses and to see his eyes express the things he couldn't say. And it was enough that he got well and was no longer in pain. This was all wine for my spirit, and I was very happy to be a part of his healing. In my unworthiness, I was enough. My failures didn't matter, only my faithfulness did.

Now, in my garden, I see something I have never seen before: Jesus is present, daily, asking *me* for a drink, asking me to bring the waters of life in my battered vessel, the only one that I own. He is asking me if I can be with him when he is the little one, the vulnerable, thirsty, hurting one, just as I ministered to Dee. If I can do this each day, despite my own feelings of unworthiness, I will be born again. My everyday water will be turned to sweet, sweet wine, and I will be fully a part of Christ's kingdom. As poet Nancy Murzyn says, Jesus will "reveal to me my inner waters of healing and renewal" and "tell me who I am."*

Perhaps the Samaritan woman knew who she was deep inside; she just needed the Special One to confirm it.

For I see the Samaritan woman differently now than I did before; this meditation has illumined her in a new way. As I

---

*Nancy Murzyn, in *Soul Weavings: A Gathering of Women's Prayers*, ed. Lyn Klug (Minneapolis: Augsburg Fortress, 1996), 63.

envision her standing beside my fountain under the shade of a big oak tree, I no longer see a beaten and forlorn woman before me; I see a *survivor*. I see a striking, strong woman who, like so many of our Bible heroines, never gave up and simply settled for sadness and resignation; against all odds she continued to hold her head high. She persistently visited the well of her salvation. In just the same way as my cracked water vessel is filled with character and beauty to me, so now I see that this woman has a beauty conceived amid all her losses.

I know that she has, in some part of her being, been waiting for just such a redeeming moment as this, just such a person as Jesus. As I reflect upon her face in my imagination, I see her gaze soften when she encounters Jesus; she knows that the moment of her rebirth has arrived. She is brave, willing to risk disappointment one more time, willing to risk it for the golden prize: a new life. She is wise and deeply intuitive; she has known many men, but this one is different; she can sense it deep within her heart. And Jesus has chosen her for just such reasons as these: she is special; she is chosen; she is to become the first apostle.

And because Jesus unmasks the call deep within her, she is able to overcome all her fears and at once go and tell all the others in her community about him, able to tell those very people who mocked and disdained her daily. I find this part of the story amazing and evidence of the mystical qualities of this encounter. It doesn't take the Samaritan woman months of therapy, years of meditation, or even days of consideration in order to act. She goes at once to others and spreads the good news; her heart is completely healed.

"Will you give me a drink?" Jesus asks, "In that damaged jug of yours? The one that is patched and worn? Yes, you; you are the one I am asking," he replies when we say, "How could *you* be asking *me* for a drink?"

"If only you really knew who is asking, if only you knew about the living water that I want to give you, you could forget your own hurts and be open and vulnerable, loving and giving. Yes, Lyn, give me a drink and I will be your drink, welling up within you, refreshing and restoring your heart. I have chosen you; you are special; I accept you fully," says Jesus, who stands near me now as a soft breeze ruffles my hair and sends acorns rolling across the patio.

"Don't be afraid," says the Samaritan woman, who also has come close. "You are accepted just as you are!" she says. "Just as I was accepted and loved and called. Come, Lyn, come! Come and see the one, *really* see the one who told me everything about myself. Come and drink of living water and pass it on to others!"

The dogs' barking at a squirrel in the lower limbs of the oak tree lifts me from my deep, prayerful musings. I think about what I have learned from this encounter, the ways this message applies to me and my life.

I remember that, centuries ago, Clement of Alexandria wrote that Christ not only gives us living water but is, in some mysterious way, the water itself. Christ is our *pege*, or living springs, an endless source that never dries and is constantly welling up within us bringing eternal life, a rich life that is present to us now. No longer must we cling to others and demand that they supply our needs; the source is within us, and it never goes dry.

After my prayer time, I understand that opportunities to be born again come to me daily from an endless Source. Thomas Keating, writing in *Heart of the World: An Introduction to Contemplative Christianity,* says that "Today each of us has a unique capacity to express Christ to the people we meet. Each of us is called by God to be an incarnation of Christ."

I record in my journal in purple crayon some of the ways I feel that oneness with God in Christ, the times that God's water flows through my life:

- *When I am willing to get out of my comfort zone and to know that despite my failings I am called by God*

- *When I admit that my anger was unjust and I apologize for acting it out*

- *When I emerge from a series of days in which I have felt sad and unwell, and realize that I am restored and happy again*

- *When I offer God gratitude for my many gifts and realize that it's all grace*

- *When I am tenderly kind to someone I don't know, and no one knows about it but the Spirit within me*

- *When I accept the littleness within myself and admit that I sometimes need a drink from others*

- *When I can walk in the world gently and remain flexible about my own plans and agendas*

- *When I refrain from joining in when another is being criticized*

- *When I give a wise and measured response to injustice and the misuse of power*

- *When I stand up for those who are abused or discounted*

- *When I realize that those I dislike have much to teach me*

- *When I give myself to others out of love, not fear or falseness*

Putting down my crayon, I look up into the sky and see the long, strong arms of the live oaks, their dark-green leaves motionless in the pale sky below the rich, whipped-cream clouds. As I pick up my small, clay-colored water vessel and turn it meditatively in my hands, a little rabbit hops out of the thicket beyond me and sits, alertly waiting, listening, and watching. I rise, set the jug down gently and turn on the hose, directing its stream of clear, cool water into the fountain, waking the fish who begin to happily spin about. Jesus and the Samaritan woman have faded into the recesses of my heart as I take up my battered jug once again, fill it with water, and pour it into the dogs' dish. Charlie and Beau slurp loudly and with gusto as they drink. I splash a bit of water on my toes, and it refreshes me.

I smile and give humble thanks to the Samaritan woman for showing me that I, too, have been chosen and baptized in the Spirit — that my water can be daily turned to wine.

—L.H.D.

## TINA'S JUG

Tina's Jug,

Are you an image of my soul?

Cracked and pieced together, with glue oozing out along
the fault lines?

Barely able to hold water,

An unlikely choice for a water bearer,

You have come to me for a reason, little jug.

When I lay my hand upon you, you are warm and
pleasing, organic in a way that a stainless steel
pitcher (which would carry water perfectly) can
never be.

You speak of life to me in the way a plastic pitcher (which
doesn't break when dropped) could never do.

I pick you up and you are heavy with the weight of living,
the depth of offering yourself up,

And trying, trying yet again.

Rusty and rough, etched with lines, subtle in colors of
ochre, rust, and red, you are

beautiful in a way the world doesn't understand. You are
made from the earth by a Maker's hand.

You are the Samaritan woman's jug and I —

I am the Samaritan woman.

—L.H.D.

# 15

# Ruth

## I Will Follow You

But Ruth said, "Entreat me not to leave you or to return from following you; for where you go I will go, and where you lodge I will
lodge; your people shall be my people, and your God my God."
—Ruth 1:16

> when the time is ripe,
> the vision will come.
> when the heart is ready,
> the fruit will appear.
> when the soul is mature,
> the harvest will happen.
>
> —Joyce Rupp,
> *Dear Heart, Come Home*

**LHD** There are few if any stories in the Bible that concern
mothers and daughters. Lots of fathers and sons
appear, but few daughters. It seems to me, however, that the
story of Ruth and Naomi *is* the story of a mother and daughter,
albeit with a twist. Ruth's story is about following after a role
model, an older caregiver and advisor who *was* mother to
her. I was struck by this fact as I began to write this book,
and I realized, now that I am in my fifties and my mother is
over eighty, that we daughters *do* follow our mothers and have

done so through the eons. We don't always expect to, or plan to, but we do; I have.

In the Bible story of Ruth, Naomi tried to send Ruth away for her own good, but the truth was that Ruth could not go. Naomi was mother to her; she was a part of Ruth's heart and Ruth would follow her, no matter the circumstances. And so Ruth said these beautiful words and so do I:

*Entreat me not to leave you, or to return from following you. Where you go; I will go.*

My own mother was an avid reader and writer, and grammar was her hobby. There were many rules about grammar in our house: Let all subjects and verbs agree in Mother's presence! May no one commit the mortal sin of the double negative! She taught me how to speak and write more than any school teacher ever did. She also wanted me to learn to play the piano (she couldn't) and swim, and she urged me to explore, to travel. "There's so much to see, so much more outside the bounds of Bastrop, Louisiana; I want you to know about the world; never stop learning," she said.

*Entreat me not to leave you, or to turn back from following you. Where you go; I will go.*

And now I write books and music, and I still swim, almost every week; I never have stopped learning. And when we go on trips and I want to spend two hours at the museum, my husband calls me "Minnetta," which is my mother's name. But I don't mind anymore, well, not much.

*Entreat me not to leave you, or to turn back from following you. Where you go; I will go.*

Ruth and Naomi were strong women, enduring the loss of all the supporting males in their lives and facing an uncertain future with bravery and faith. They lived through extremely stressful times, and I wonder whether there were quarrels not recorded in the sacred pages. My own mother is a strong woman (as I have been told I am also), and we sometimes had trouble understanding one another. We got lost in silences and things we dared not say. She was a protective mother tiger, and I saw only the tiger. She tried to control the events and people around her, and a big part of me felt I couldn't be myself in her presence. She wanted to mold me well so that I would be successful; I was hurt by her criticisms and frightened of her moods. Mother got lost in her own pain at times, and so did I. No one could ever upset me the way she did, with just a few words, and yet, no one was prouder of me than she was. She regretfully told me in a letter once, "I wish I had praised my children more." Now my memories of her come back, gentled and lightened. My heart continues to repeat Ruth's words as I remember things about my mother:

*Entreat me not to leave you, or to return from following you. Where you go; I will go.*

My mother encouraged me to have fun, go waterskiing, go to parties, and enjoy college life at LSU. I think whatever fun my mother had in her life, which encompassed the Great Depression and a world war, was hard won. She wanted me to have good friends, and most of all, a good husband.

Naomi, Ruth's mother-in-law, led her to a new marriage in another land. My own mother's marriage was her joy in life, and she worried greatly about who her children and grand-children might marry, and she was right. Marriage can be a passage to deep contentment or can earn its partners sad-ness and despair. I have been married happily for thirty-five years. It's not perfect, but it is often really, really good, just like my parents' marriage still is after sixty-five years (even as they grow more and more frail and their hold on life weak-ens). Mother's unspoken message was, "Value your marriage, cherish it, and take care of it." I never thought about these things before; perhaps I am growing in wisdom. Perhaps after so many years of being maddened by her, I finally understand that all things work together for good eventually; they really do.

*Entreat me not to leave you; or to return from following you. Where you go; I will go.*

Naomi of the Bible lost all of her children, except her daughter-in-law Ruth, who truly became her own daughter. There must have been much pain in Naomi's heart; indeed, she was led to call herself "Mara, the bitter one." I remember the day thirty-five years ago when I left for LSU, the fall before my impending marriage at Christmas. We were all sitting around the dining room table, and suddenly it hit both my mother and me: I would not be coming back home in the same way, ever again. Her eyes reddened and filled with tears and so did mine. I understand only now how different her loss was from mine. My life was just beginning; all was new. For my mother, I was the third daughter to move away. I wonder now; I wonder what my mother really felt.

*Entreat me not to leave you, or to return from following you. Where you go; I will go.*

Naomi brought Ruth into her religion, the worship of the one God. My mother was the first one to take me to Sunday school, and we often went to church as a family when I was growing up. Then she stopped going; I never found out why. This was an example of the many things we couldn't talk about. But that's okay; she had her path, I had mine — they touched, they wound together, they diverged. It's odd, but because of my parents' lack of religiosity, I have almost no religious guilt. In that area, I am free and I can share that freedom with those I counsel. I have other kinds of guilt, but little surrounds the matters of religion. I don't recommend religious indifference as a path for parents; it's just interesting the healthy way it worked out for me.

And now I look in the mirror, and I see my mother's brown eyes looking back at me. Like her, I love warm colors and avocados and hot dogs — the way she made them with tons of stuff on top — and I have too many clothes in my closet and a messy refrigerator that looks much like hers. I hardly ever follow recipes and neither did she, yet people loved her cooking and they like mine a lot too.

Naomi taught Ruth to follow after the gleaners, and in this way Ruth began to procure a new life in addition to bread. The recipes were simple in biblical days, but they were life-giving and life-saving in ways we can only begin to understand. Ruth would have been lost without Naomi's guidance. I can now celebrate my own mother's influence on me as well, because I have changed, because now I understand things in a different way.

*Entreat me not to leave you, or to return from following
you. Where you go; I will go.*

My mother and father now live in an assisted-living facility,
and their recent, rapid decline has forced me to face my own
mortality with seriousness. It's been a sad struggle for Mother
to grow old and especially to leave her beloved home. Ruth
and Naomi both experienced displacement, this loss of home,
and I wonder now about myself. How long will I live on five
intensely green acres under sheltering oaks? This is the very
stuff of faith, I find, the nuts and bolts of living and dying.
But it is in smaller things and shared moments that I feel my
mother's influence so deeply.

*Entreat me not to leave you, or to return from following
you. Where you go; I will go.*

Such an occasion occurred recently when I visited my parents
at their new apartment and we all went out onto the porch:
my parents and my daddy's caregiver, Karen, and me. As we
sat there in the sunlight, I said, "Mom, your fingernail polish
looks almost like mine."

"Yes, it does," she said. "They just took me to get my nails
done."

"What is your color?" Karen asked me.

"It's called Twenty Candles on a Birthday Cake," I said. "I
learned the name because I want to get it again."

"Yep, that's her color, too," said Karen. "Twenty Candles, I
remember."

I was a little stunned; my mother and I, living hundreds of
miles from each other and selecting among dozens of colors

of polish — at different manicurists' shops — had chosen *the exact same shade.*

*Entreat me not to leave you, or to return from following you. Where you go; I will go.*

It seems like such a small thing, but it was not.

As Ruth of the Bible harvested grain at Naomi's urging and learned to recast her life in a new land, I now harvest the gold of healed memories and changed impressions. I finally understand my mother much better — the ways I am like her and the ways I am not. It is peaceful to follow after her in some ways as I recognize that in other ways I resemble her not at all. Finally, after so many years, I am at peace with the mother that will always live on in my heart.

*And on that certain day, in the rosy and fading light, my mother and I held our orangey-red-tipped fingers up together and admired them, as night approached and our hearts beat with the steady rhythm of the cicada's call. Perhaps I heard Ruth and Naomi's muted footsteps as they rounded the corner, just out of sight, and slipped away together into the warm summer darkness.*

—L.H.D.

# 16

# Hannah

## Help Me to Relinquish My Own Desires

And she said, "Oh, my lord! As you live, my lord, I am the woman who was standing here in your presence, praying to the Lord. For this child I prayed; and the Lord has granted me the petition that I made to him. Therefore I have lent him to the Lord; as long as he lives, he is given to the Lord." She left him there for the Lord.

—1 Samuel 1:27–28

Well, there is a time to let go of our dearest, and with every letting go, we take a step closer to the inner freedom for which we have been created. Our love is purified from any attachment thus becoming more and more like the Life-giving Love that is the source of all creatures, including us. Such a big mystery. Living is sharing what we receive and giving what is not really ours to keep!

—Father Paul Chetcuti, S.J.

For my progress in living out my life in Christ will be in proportion to the surrender of my own self-love and of my own will and interests.

—David Fleming, *Draw Me into Your Friendship*

**RH** A couple of summers ago I led a book study group, which I often do as part of my ministry at the Catholic church where I am employed as a spiritual director. A friend had introduced me to the text *A Woman after God's Own Heart*, a book that had offered her practical insights on how to best pursue God's priorities in her life. Moved by her testimony, I decided to use the text for a summer book journey, an eight-week

series for female college students and women of our parish. A
lovely community gathered on Monday mornings that summer,
every woman in her unique way seeking after God's own heart.

Preparing for our gatherings involved not only reading ahead
in the text, but planning for the prayer time that would begin
each session. This communal prayer was a special part of our
sharing and drew our hearts together every week, creating a sacred space in which we could glean wisdom from one another's
prayerful insights. When planning the program, I had decided
to choose biblical women as models for our journey, trusting
that we could blend parts of their stories with elements of our
own. We enjoyed many living experiences with those women
and with each other that summer, an experience that partially
birthed this book, as explained in our introduction.

I remember the night I chose Hannah for an upcoming session. Sitting on my bed one Sunday evening like a student doing
her homework at the end of the weekend, I read the next chapter
of our book. While choosing our next prayed-with sister from
the Bible, my favorite part of the planning, I felt drawn to check
the Scripture selections for Mass the next day. I delightfully discovered the perfect woman for our prayer time in Monday's first
reading. In the first book of Samuel I read the moving story of
Samuel's mother, Hannah, and felt a connection with her from
an earlier time in my life. I had come upon a cherished friend.

I recalled the first time I had ever prayed with Hannah. Her
story had strengthened me one morning when I was working
desperately to surrender my future with my husband, Easton.
In her grief over her barrenness, I had seen my own — the un-
fruitfulness that occurs when I attempt to control my life. I

remembered how deeply I had desired the graces she had received — those of faith, trust, and surrender. I wanted to pursue God the way she had. I desired to be able to give him back every gift he had ever blessed me with, yet felt far from that possibility. Through her striking example of strength and faith, I had felt moved to pray so very hard for a full surrender of all of my desires.

I slowly reread her story, allowing its impact to speak to my journey again that evening. Different facets of the story stood out for me this time. Her pleading reminded me of the many times that I plead with God, the tears I shed when praying, especially when I'm caught in a struggle, feeling unfruitful and helpless. I noticed for the first time how Hannah stood meekly in her own truth and tender need in the face of Eli's misjudgment. I thought of how often I want to defend myself in the reality of misunderstanding, focusing on the needs of my ego, instead of my deepest self. Thinking back over my journey since the first time I had prayed with Hannah, I reflected on the many times in my life that I have felt attached to an outcome and desperate in my search for it. I thought of a husband, a house, a marriage, even a silly piece of furniture, and yes, a child. I noted how in every circumstance, prying apart my clinging fingers had brought the surprise of something wonderful and amazingly new, accompanied by internal freedom and greater trust in God. I couldn't wait to share my friend with the others, to bring Hannah with me to our gathering the next morning.

As always, a sacred tenderness was present among the journeying women. Hearts were touched by Hannah's inner knowing that everything we have is a gift from God, including our children, who are not our possessions to begin with.

The gathered mothers admitted their tendency to hang on to that which is God's in the first place. Admiration spilled over for Hannah not only for having a proper set of values, but for being able to actively follow through with them and not renege on her promise. We all left that meeting strengthened by our living experience with our new sister.

The power of Hannah's story continued to impact me during the Mass that followed our gathering. I wasn't surprised that Father Joe McGill, S.J., who was celebrating our liturgy, preached on the touching story in Samuel. Father McGill is a gifted story-teller, and I am always moved by his narratives. Often based on his own life, they are the kind you never forget because you can easily imagine yourself right in the story.

That day he told an amazing account of his own experience as a sort of baby Samuel and the relinquishment his mother faced when at age one, he had spiked a high fever that the doctor couldn't cure. Not willing to abandon the listless baby boy, his determined godmother sought a priest to come pray over the child, requesting that he bring along a relic of Saint Anne de Beaupré, the mother of Mary. Father McGill's godmother was very devoted to Saint Anne and believed that the saint could intercede for the baby. The visiting cleric dismissed the family and proceeded to pray and apply the relic to the child. When the nursery door eventually opened, the women found little Joseph standing in his crib, his ear draining from a severe inner ear infection, his fever gone. God had cured him, but God would also use Joseph's life for his own purposes. Months later, Father McGill's mother, Anna, along with his godmother, took her son to church for a visit with the priest. Anna desired to give her child's life to God because God had given her baby's life back to her. She approached the altar and handed her son to the vested priest, surrendering Joseph to God. It wasn't until four years after Father McGill was an ordained Jesuit priest that he discovered his mother's brave act of surrender, explaining his mysterious call to a religious order that required intense study, which he had never been fond of doing. He is now seventy-six years old and still preaching and inspiring his congregations with stories from a life full of service and surrender. It was nice to know a real live Samuel with a genuine Hannah mother. I liked Anna's spirit as much as I liked Hannah's. (I find it interesting that even their names are almost identical!) I had never considered offering my children to God and thought that perhaps it wasn't too late, even though they were now grown.

This morning I prayed again with Hannah. I needed the model of her strength for a situation involving a change at work that required my surrender, even though I've come to realize that surrender is never required, it is merely offered as part of the journey for treasured freedom. I desired the freedom to stop fighting the changes I was facing. No matter how many times I have, through grace, been able to force open my gripping hands, it seems to never get easier, and I forget that surrender itself is a grace, a gift from God. And so in my pain I turned to the experts for help and first read about Jesus in the Garden of Gethsemane in Matthew's Gospel, a story steeped in relinquishment, a theme in Hannah's struggle and now in my own. I prayed with the holy account of his agony and read about Jesus's sadness and despair. Imagining *his* anguish gave me permission to feel my own. I too wept and asked Jesus to be with me in my suffering.

Then I read the account of Hannah. I needed a sister, a woman to share in my hurt, a model of one who turned her own despair into a heartfelt prayer:

*Hannah rose and presented herself before the Lord....She was deeply distressed and prayed to the Lord and wept bitterly.*  — I Samuel 1:9

I felt strengthened by Hannah's decision not to be a victim of circumstances and to go to God instead in her misery. She had suffered disgrace as a woman because of her infertility and because of another woman, her husband's other wife no less! Hannah took her desperate heart straight to the Healer of Hearts, the only one who could grant her deepest desires. I too poured out my heart to God, though my own predicament seemed ridiculously trite compared to hers. I knew deep down, however, that no situation is beyond the power of God's grace, beyond his mercy and tender care. I begged him to answer my prayer, and then I read on.

*She made this vow: "O Lord of hosts, if only you will look on the misery of your servant, and remember me, and not forget your servant, but will give to your servant a male child, then I will set him before you as a nazirite until the day of his death."*  — I Samuel 1:11

Recognizing that she first consecrated to God the very thing she wanted the most, it seemed that Hannah had the key to all of our desires — that anything we long for must be surrendered first. I prayed to God, offering to him the outcome I desired the most. Everything I want is all his anyway. I am just a vessel of his love. I prayed to accept his will and to carry his love with me in my difficult situation.

> *And she said, "Oh, my lord! As you live, my lord, I am the woman who was standing here in your presence, praying to the Lord. For this child I prayed; and the Lord has granted me the petition that I made to him. Therefore I have lent him to the Lord; as long as he lives, he is given to the Lord." She left him there for the Lord.*                    — I Samuel 1:26–28

Gripped once again by Hannah's obedience to a vow — a vow she had initiated on her own — I thought of my own struggle with obedience. I saw my reluctance to give my own authority to another. Looking closer, I recognized that Hannah's vow was a mature response to a call that God had placed within her, one she had felt deeply the day she had pleaded with God. She wasn't merely doing what she was told to do. She was responding to a call within her own heart. Her obedience drew forth my own, as part of my present struggle had to do with deferring my own desires to a person of authority in my life. I recognized finally that the obedience I was called to was a truth within my own heart, where God seemed to be saying to me, "Let go. Let go as Hannah did. Trust me." I prayed once again for the grace of surrender and finally felt free.

> *Hannah prayed and said, "My heart exults in the Lord; my strength is exalted in my God. My mouth derides my enemies, because I rejoice in my victory. There is no Holy One like the Lord, no one besides you; there is no Rock like our God."*
>                    — I Samuel 2:1–2

I now shared in Hannah's strength and deep gratitude. This morning, I knew what she had known. I felt God's love with a deep awareness that he would provide in the way he saw fit, even if my prayer was not fulfilled as I'd hoped. The answered prayer would come in freedom, the deep-down peace obtained through obedience to authority, not just human authority, but an inner authority that comes from the divine.

HANNAH, YOU ACCOMPLISHED the utterly incredible task of giving back to God the most cherished possession of your life, your son, and in that profound act of relinquishment gave strength to all women as we each struggle to give back to God our firmly held treasures. I feel privileged to have come to know you so much better. You have given voice to my struggles and offered me hope — hope that the depth of my desires can touch the depths of God's heart, too. I thank you my sister, my friend, for the encouragement I have drawn from you so many times. I thank you for showing me the way.                    —R.H.

# 17

# The Bent-Over Woman

## I Was Lifted Up

Now he was teaching in one of the synagogues on the sabbath.

And there was a woman who had had a spirit of infirmity for eighteen years; she was bent over and could not fully straighten herself.

And when Jesus saw her, he called her and said to her, "Woman, you are freed from your infirmity."

And he laid his hands upon her, and immediately she was made straight, and she praised God.

But the ruler of the synagogue, indignant because Jesus had healed on the sabbath, said to the people, "There are six days on which work ought to be done; come on those days and be healed, and not on the sabbath day."

Then the Lord answered him, "You hypocrites! Does not each of you on the sabbath untie his ox or his ass from the manger, and lead it away to water it?

"And ought not this woman, a daughter of Abraham whom Satan bound for eighteen years, be loosed from this bond on the sabbath day?" As he said this, all his adversaries were put to shame; and all the people rejoiced at all the glorious things that were done by him.

— Luke 13:10–17

Proclaim Jubilee! We as women are being called by God to stand straight, to stand tall!

— Sister Mary Lou Cranston, speech, May 22, 2000

Surely / You meant / when You lifted / her up / Long ago / To your praise, / Compassionate One, / not one woman / only / but all women / bent / by unbending ways.

— Miriam Therese Winter, *Soul Weavings*

LHD This summer, when the sugar cane was high, thick, and green, and the air was misty with humidity, I prayed deeply with the women of the Bible. One afternoon I took the opportunity to sit on my porch, light a candle, and read the account of the Bent-Over Woman from Luke's Gospel. As I read about the woman who had been painfully bent over for eighteen years — such a long time! — and then was healed by Jesus, I began to form a picture of her in my mind. As I thought about her, I slowly visualized the scene in the synagogue on the day of her healing. Behind my closed eyes, I saw the stones of the temple, shifting shadows thrown by torches on the walls, and then her, a woman bent far over and shuffling toward Jesus.

In my imagination, I asked the Bent-Over Woman to speak to me and tell me what was binding her. Her face was pinched and gray as she looked at me and spoke with difficulty. She told me that her body had betrayed her, that it was bent with pain and sadness. When I asked her how she had become ill, she paused. As I looked at her in my mind's eye, I saw that she was deeply repressed in spirit, mind, and body. The struggle to be a woman in her day, and her culture's refusal to let her truly be herself, had overwhelmed her. Her sadness and pain had expressed itself in her body to the extent that she was almost doubled over. As I pondered her, a personal memory came back to me, clearly and in great detail. It was a period when I was a bent-over woman, a walking symbol of repression.

Years ago, when my husband, Dee, and I were raising Jacques, I was teaching special education at an inner-city school. I was ill and I was frightened about how ill I felt. My symptoms included extreme fatigue that haunted my days, two panic attacks, frequent dizziness, a twitching little finger (I remember that as being the scariest symptom), and an overwhelming sadness that I hid under a bright smile and didn't admit, even to myself.

As I looked back on this time in my life, I realized that I, too, like the Bent-Over Woman, had severely repressed feelings and personality. My energy was swallowed up in tenseness as I tried to be perfectly pleasing to all and do the impossible. I was dealing with severely impaired children with behavior problems in my classroom, and with daily discipline challenges on the playground and in the halls of my school. There were also the personality conflicts and problems between employees that happen at every workplace. Our staff was large and we had to work very closely together to provide the needed services to our handicapped kids. I lost any sense of having choices and felt compelled, all the time, to give 110 percent to the outside world at the expense of my self.

As Sarah Ban Breathnach says in *Something More*, "Our choices can be conscious or unconscious. Conscious choice is creative, the heart of authenticity. Unconscious choice is destructive, the heel of self-abuse."*

As I continued to live with my unconscious choices, I remained severely depressed over the great gap I saw between my real (hidden) self and the idealized self that I wanted to be: a perfect (or at least very outstanding) wife, mother, and teacher. In the process of seeking this idealized but false self, I adopted so many rigid roles and behaviors that I lost *myself*, my real self, just a regular person with needs, wants, and all

---

*Sarah Ban Breathnach, *Something More: Excavating Your Authentic Self* (New York: Warner Books, 1998), 41.

sorts of feelings. As I honed my people-pleasing skills and beat myself up over every perceived failing, my body and inner spirit rebelled more and more. I needed Jesus's help, I really did.

I returned from my memories to my prayer with the Bent-Over Woman, and I wrote this in my journal:

*Ah, my Bible sister, what was it that hurt your body? Too many children born to you? The lowest place at the table? For eighteen years you lived looking only at the ground. What kept you hoping and living for all those years?*

In my mind I heard her whisper, "My hope came from the Lord, who made heaven and earth."

And suddenly I saw in this crippled soul a strength that was deep and true, forged in a fire of pain, like a blue diamond, like steel. She still had the desire to live fully, and be joyful; it was a desire set in her heart by the Spirit, and it called her forth to begin a brand-new life on a fateful day.

I recognized her strength in myself. For I never gave up either. I knew that I had a great capacity for happiness as well as for sadness, and I wanted with all my heart to be well and strong. Jesus came to me, as he did to her, but in many disguises. I wasn't healed in one fell swoop, as she was, but over the course of months and years.

As I pondered my healing those years ago, I remembered Maddie, a young massage therapist whom I saw weekly for a while at the urging of a good friend. One day as I approached the therapy room, she gently touched my shoulders with her hands, pulling on them slightly. "My goodness. I think you are trying to cover your heart with your shoulders. That must hurt after a while!" Weekly, she teased the knots out of my body with her strong hands, and, as poet Kay Ryan says, "Each touch uncatches some remote lock." As the mysteries of my muscle pain unlocked and released, I cried from deep within. Maddie encouraged this, saying that I was shedding "old stuff." "It all lodges in your body," she said. "The body never forgets."

As I remembered Maddie, and her touch, I spoke to the Bent-Over One in my prayer:

> *Bent-Over Woman, what was your body trying to forget? Had you run out of choices? Had the ones you loved left you? Were you filled with feelings of low worth, with the sadness of a hundred rejections? Were you trapped in the past? They didn't even give you a name! Who wants to be called "Bent-Over Woman"? How did you feel when Jesus said, "Come forth"? Could you have known that not only your body but your whole self would be healed? That you would get a new name, "Daughter of Abraham"?*

Like the Bent-Over Woman, my physical illness was to be the catalyst that would bring me total healing of body, mind, and spirit. Jesus would come to me in many ways to offer new life.

Jesus once came to me during this time disguised as an internist (who spoke little and whom I didn't like at all!). After I had spent much time and money on tests, he suggested only iron tablets and counseling. "He thinks this physical distress is all in my mind," I sputtered. But the next week, in a therapist's office, I began to learn about my unconscious strivings and the harsh inner voices (therapists call them introjections) that were ruling my life and forcing my body to react. Thinking back on this, I remembered my insecurities and my lack of freedom to be who I really was, although the healthy part of me was calling me to embrace that very freedom. A house divided against itself really can't stand, I discovered.

I learned some of the reasons why I was the way I was when I looked at the environmental and social mores that I had unconsciously swallowed: women were still encouraged to be submissive to the needs of others and to repress their feelings in order to keep peace. Humility, a wonderful Christian virtue, was not being practiced equally by everyone in my life, as it should have been, allowing me to be victimized. Unfortunately, this will always happen, but awareness can help one deal with it and avoid the victim role. Also, I had been put into situations where I had much responsibility, but little power, a surefire recipe for psychic distress. Some of these conditions I could do little about, but others I could work to remedy.

I began to unravel my idealized self, the self that everyone approved of, and I realized that she had never existed, except in my own mind. And that was a good thing, because she wasn't human. Jesus came to me as I went on retreats where I encountered wonderful, life-giving retreat directors and guides who taught me about being an assertive Christian and giving myself the care I gave to others. I embraced the parables and healing stories of the Gospels, and I began to fall in love with Jesus and with life in a new way.

I read books about people who had encountered the same difficulties that I had and absorbed new ways to live. Jesus touched me through prayer, journaling, and inner work as the months passed, and I slowly uncovered my true self — the one God had made — and I began to accept her and even to like her.

I began to get well, and my physical symptoms fell away.

I learned new strengths as I sought to live in the present; I was no longer stuck in the past or the future. As my internal world changed, I actualized it in the outer world and began to make strong, conscious choices. I applied for a sabbatical from my teaching job and went back to graduate school. I let music, which I loved, more fully into my life, and I wrote songs, poems, and prayers and studied *The Artist's Way.* I eventually got a much calmer job at a small school. I began to take long walks several times a week, and I continued to get massages.

I still often tried to be perfect, but I was much more in touch with who I really was; I became less afraid that others would find me unpleasing. I uncovered my true gifts of writing, speaking, and facilitating women's groups. For most of us, the journey of transformation is just that: a journey. And it never really ends. At this point in my life, I think that is good news indeed.

As my journey continued, I sought training as a spiritual director, and now I study to be a therapist because I want to help other women stand tall and make the inner journeys that they are called to make. I believe so deeply that God calls us to lives of joy and fulfillment. Like the Bent-Over Woman, we are all called to stand tall and to use the gifts we have been given.

I MET THE Bent-Over Woman again in prayer after our initial encounter. Together, we spun a tale of her life after her healing, and I wrote it down in my journal. She was still somewhat young when she was healed, and she married and had a daughter whom she brought with her to the market, where they both walked straight and strong. She sewed beautiful things because she loved to, sitting in the sunlight under an olive tree, watching her beautiful and bright little daughter as she played with her dolls. She saw Jesus one more time in the Temple Square and gave him a small, beautifully embroidered linen napkin in gratitude. She wonders if it lay near the bread and wine at his final meal. She wonders if Jesus touched the cloth even once and remembered *her* — the woman he healed and called, "Daughter of Abraham."

> *You, Daughter of Abraham, live on in my heart now, a timeless symbol of the love of God, a messenger of hope, health, life, and new beginnings. I close my eyes, and you smile at me in health and happiness, and we celebrate — because Jesus is so alive in both our hearts.*
>
> —L.H.D.

We come to the end of our journey of story and we hope you will enjoy the study guide to follow. We pray that you will embrace, or continue to embrace, a new life of standing tall in faith. The poem "Daughters of Abraham" is dedicated to you, our treasured readers.

## DAUGHTERS OF ABRAHAM

Daughters of Abraham, come forth!
Move forward and leave behind all that has held you
     bound,
the falseness and conformity that has filled your bodies
     with pain,
Bending you over until you couldn't see.

Cast it away now,
Like the dried husks of locusts, a snakeskin left behind,
You emerge shiny-new, multicolored and real,
Larger and growing larger still.

Daughters of Abraham,
Dance!
Drenched by the waters of Sabbath on new skin,
Standing tall and lifting arms in praise,
Called forward, called forth, called in joy for freedom's joy.
Beautiful, wonderful, Daughters of Abraham.
Dance!                    —L.H.D.

# Study Guide

## ～⁓ *Transformation* ⁓～
## *with the Biblical Women*

### *A First Step*

Many women express a hunger for a sacred space where deep authentic connecting can occur between kindred spirits, where holy listening can take place and solid discernment can become clear. For over two decades, I have gathered with and among women, young and old, in a prayerful setting to offer a rhythm that complements our inherent understanding of cycles — daily, weekly, monthly — where, for a short while, we stop striving. We relax, release, exhale, and just *are* in the presence of our own and other sacred souls. This time is a spiritual oasis, a little sabbath. A lot can happen in an hour or so. One group of dedicated women gathered weekly with me for over six years to share the journey. My Theresian community has joined together monthly for twenty-three years. Time is suspended while we partake in each other's lives. We leave the sacred circle more equipped to face the world once again.

Father Richard Rohr calls this space *liminal,* defined as a "voluntary displacement for the sake of transformation of consciousness, perspective and heart."* Choosing the threshold that liminal space presents is a first step in transformation, an opportunity we are offering with this guide.

## A Second Step

A second step in transformation is what I call "listening for the stirrings." A stirring is a slight movement, a "catch," even an agitation, perhaps an arousal that occurs in the heart or the belly in response to an image or words. Sometimes the movement is so slight we call it a tiny whispering sound, as did Elijah in the Book of Kings. It is one of the ways God speaks to us. When stirrings occur, God has entered, and we stop to pay attention. That's what we do in group process: we listen for the stirrings inside as we partake in prayer, read Scripture or other holy readings, and listen to one another, taking note of the invitation to open up our unexamined inner realms. As the stirrings occur, we respond by internally asking:

*Lord, what are you saying? Where does the finger of this word, phrase, or image touch my life? What about my life, Lord, are you affirming, challenging, or inviting me to heal?*

We look to see if there is pain to be expressed or joy to be shared. Regardless of where we are, we experience a comfort in knowing that the Lord is with us, inviting us to examine our lives a bit closer so that he can better partake in them. In group process, there is also a reassurance from others who share in our journey.

---

*Richard Rohr, *Everything Belongs: The Gift of Contemplative Prayer* (New York: Crossroad, 1999), 48.

## A Third Step

A third step in transformation involves defining and declaring the action we are being called to take and then committing to taking it. Here's where the accountability of a group can be a prized possession. We make a promise to ourselves and to others, knowing that it will be upheld and that we will be supported in love, even if we fail.

## A Final Thought

The language of the soul has one expression: love. Whenever I gather with my Mexican sisters during my mission work in Mexico, we understand each other well, with or without translators. Who can't comprehend the meaning of a tear, a heartfelt prayer, a tender hug, even a foreign language when spoken from the soul? Perhaps the most powerful benefit of community has nothing to do with the reading material and everything to do with the *love* that is shared through the commitment to be present to one another, anam ċaras along the journey. We bid you well in your gatherings.      —R.H.

## ❧ *Lectio Divina* ❧ *Shared in Community*

*Lectio Divina,* "divine reading," is an ancient spiritual art of prayer that is being rediscovered in our day, resurrected from the desert fathers and kept alive by the Benedictine monks. It is a way of allowing the Scriptures to become again what God intended that they should be — a means of uniting us to himself. As the monks conceived it, *Lectio Divina* is not used for the sake of information, but for insight. It is not used to learn something, but to encounter Christ. Applying *Lectio Divina* to a group process involves four steps:

1. *Lectio:* Reading and Listening

   Quiet yourselves before the Lord.

   One person reads the Scripture passage slowly.

   Sit in silence and listen to the inner stirrings in your heart. Allow a certain word or phrase to catch your attention.

   Share aloud the word(s) you "heard" without elaboration.

2. *Meditatio:* Meditation

   Another person reads the passage slowly again.

   Sit quietly and meditate on the stirrings. This is the time for "pondering in your heart."

   Reflect on where and how the words touch your life today.

   Share aloud briefly, "I am hearing ... "

3. *Oratio:* Prayer

   A third person reads the passage, slowly again.

   Again become quiet and pray with the stirrings you experienced. This is the time for dialogue with God.

   Listen for what God is calling you to at this time in your life.

   Share aloud with the group, "I believe that God is asking me to ... "

4. *Contemplatio:* Contemplation

If there is time, another person reads the passage once more.

Allow time for simply being in the presence of God and one another.

After a few moments of silence, conclude with the Our Father.

## ᘗᘐᘚᓬ *Praying with Scripture* ᘚᘐᓬᘗ *and Imagination*

Using imaginative prayer in a group is enjoyable and not difficult. Here are some steps to follow:

1. Use the Scriptures suggested for each story in the study guide.

2. Light a candle and have everyone quiet down with gentle breathing. Have someone say an opening prayer such as the following: *Dear God, Holy Spirit, as we pray with your sacred word today, open our spirits to its message. Make your Scripture real in our hearts. Teach us what you would have us learn, and fill us with your knowledge and your love. Amen.*

3. Choose one person to read the chosen Bible story aloud, as each person in the group closes her or his eyes and allows the message to penetrate at a heart level. Do this slowly and prayerfully.

4. Have a different person in the group read the Bible story again, as each person in the group begins to visualize the place and the people as well as the action of the story. For example, is the day dusty and hot? Are the people eager, angry or joyful? What colors are there? What elements in the story stand out? What people? What are the high points in the action of the story? How could you have participated in the action if you had lived in that day?

5. Now each person closes his or her eyes and clearly visualizes the scene again in silence. Some groups like to play soft, meditative music at this time. Each person in the group will try at this point to put herself or himself in the story. The listener imagines being one of the main characters, an onlooker, a servant, or anyone else. Now, everyone tries to imagine the entire story clearly. Follow the story to its ending. Here's a tricky part: try not to over-control the experience. Surprising things may start to happen; release any preconceived notions and flow in the river of the prayer.

6. Allow a few minutes for personal reflection. Have each person sit quietly and reflect: In your imagination how did you respond to Jesus and to others? Did you talk to anyone? (For example, when I, Lyn, entered the scene of Jesus's birth in a deep prayer experience, I was able to talk with Joseph, learning much about the state of his heart, his worries, and his love for Mary. I have loved Joseph more deeply ever since that experience.) Note what you are feeling, as your feeling state is very important in this process, but don't strain to feel anything in particular.

7. Share with one another what happened during this scriptural prayer experience. Be thorough but brief so that everyone can share.

8. Have someone close with a prayer she likes, or say the following prayer together: *Holy Spirit, thank you for coming to be with us today in our prayer. We love you, and we know that your Being enlivens Holy Scripture. Jesus, thank you for the privilege of walking with you and learning to love you more. Amen.*

## 1. Mary and Elizabeth

**Pray and meditate** on Luke 1:39–45.

**Follow** the steps in Lectio Divina or Praying with Scripture and Imagination.

**Reflect** on the essay "Blessed Am I Among Women" and the poem "Elizabeth."

**Journal and/or share:**

- Who have been the significant anam ċaras in my life? How has my life been enhanced by them?

- Exploring the women friendships I have today, what are the challenges? The blessings?

- What do my most life-enhancing visitations look like?

**Listen** for the name of a significant anam ċara in your life today.

**Write** a letter thanking her for her presence, for the contribution she has made to your life. Consider mailing it.

## 2. Martha _____

**Pray and meditate** on Luke 10:38–42.

**Follow** the steps in Lectio Divina or Praying with Scripture and Imagination.

**Reflect** on the essay "I Discovered the One Thing."

**Journal and/or share:**

- What are some boundaries that can protect me from overextending myself?

- What are some expectations I have for myself that are linked to other people's expectations of me?

- When I am like Martha with God's help, what changes in my attitudes and my behavior do I seek?

- What greater simplicity might God be calling me to?

**Listen** for God's voice beckoning to spend time with you in prayer.

**Write** a prayer seeking God's help to enable you to do so.

## 3. Martha _____

**Pray and meditate** on Luke 10:38–42 and John 12:1–2.

**Follow** the steps in Lectio Divina or Praying with Scripture and Imagination.

**Reflect** on the essay "I Want the Better Part."

**Journal and/or share:**

- What are some of the components of my divided heart? When is my heart most divided?

- What were the results of a time when my "yes" was clearly God's "yes"?

- When is my service most joyous? What does that tell me?

- According to Frederick Buechner, *"The place where God calls you is the place where your deep gladness and the world's deep hunger meet."* What might that place be for me?

**Listen** for God's thank-you for all that you do.

**Write** a prayer asking God what more he wants from you.

## 4. Mary of Bethany

**Pray and meditate** on Luke 10:38–42.

**Follow** the steps in Lectio Divina or Praying with Scripture and Imagination.

**Reflect** on the essay "How Could You Love a Woman Like Me?"

**Journal and/or share:**

- How have some of my personality traits both blessed me and dismayed me at times?

- How would I describe Mary of Bethany as I imagine her to be?

- What issues, if any, do I struggle with that others don't seem to be as concerned about?

- When and how do I "go to the Source," when I am troubled about life's ups and downs?

- In what ways has my faith and courage to be myself increased over the years?

**Listen** for God's voice assuring you that you are loved, just as you are.

**Write** a prayer of thanksgiving that you are who you are.


## 5. *The Canaanite Woman* _____

**Pray and meditate** on Matthew 15:21–28.

**Follow** the steps in Lectio Divina or Praying with Scripture and Imagination.

**Reflect** on the essay "Lord, Help Me."

**Journal and/or share:**

- What situation in my life bears the greatest challenge?

- As I think of one person whom I dislike, what are the qualities that I find distasteful in them? Where are those traits found in me?

- What in me needs healing?

**Listen** for God offering you healing.

**Write** a prayer of thanksgiving as you receive his healing touch.

## 6. Sarah

**Pray and meditate** on Genesis 16:1–15 and Genesis 17:15.

**Follow** the steps in Lectio Divina or Praying with Scripture and Imagination.

**Reflect** on the essay "Why Can't I Have a Baby?" and the poem "Sarah."

**Journal and/or share:**

- When and how have I desperately longed for something that did not come to pass? What was my relationship with God like at that time?

- In what ways has God helped me to become reconciled to lost dreams or sad times in my life?

- How have I been changed by loss, disappointment, grief?

- How have I been deeply surprised by a joyful happening or period of life?

**Listen** to God giving you a new name.

**Write** a prayer-poem about your new name.

## 7. Mary Magdalene

**Pray and meditate** on John 20:1–18.

**Follow** the steps in Lectio Divina or Praying with Scripture and Imagination.

**Reflect** on the essay "It's Time for Me to Let Go."

**Journal and/or share:**

- To what and/or whom am I clinging?

- When have I encountered Jesus?

- What new mission might be calling out to me?

**Listen** for Jesus inviting you to move forward in your life.

**Write** a prayer of response to the call.

## 8. *Mary of Magdala* _____

**Pray and meditate** on Luke 8:1–3 and Luke 24:6–10.

**Follow** the steps in Lectio Divina or Praying with Scripture and Imagination.

**Reflect** on the essay "Da Vinci, Ya Never Knew Me."

**Journal and/or share:**

- What is my perception of Mary Magdalene, and has it changed recently?

- In what ways am I like her? Unlike her?

- How does knowing Mary Magdalene deepen my appreciation of Jesus?

**Listen** to Jesus calling you to be an apostle as Mary Magdalene was.

**Write** a short paragraph describing yourself as Jesus's apostle. (Hints: What gifts of service are you providing to the world, and how do you show Jesus to others?)

## 9. The Prodigal Daughter _____

**Pray and meditate** on Luke 15:11–32.

**Follow** the steps in Lectio Divina or Praying with Scripture and Imagination.

**Reflect** on the essay "I Want to Go Home."

**Journal and/or share:**

- What has my own homecoming looked like, or am I not *home* yet?

- How do I dissipate my energies?

- What are the compulsions that I use to deaden my fears?

**Listen** for the invitation God is issuing to you to come home.

**Write** a prayer responding to the invitation.

## 10. The Baker Woman _____

**Pray and meditate** on Matthew 13:33.

**Follow** the steps in Lectio Divina or Praying with Scripture and Imagination.

**Reflect** on the essay "I Bring Bread to the World."

**Journal and/or share:**

- In what ways do I share a table with others at home or elsewhere?

- Do I like to cook and bake?

- What stories of baking or cooking do I remember?
- What images does the word "bread" bring to mind?
- In what ways do I bring bread, either literally or figuratively, to the world?

**Listen** to God speaking when you gather with others around a table.

**Write** down a favorite recipe and share it with others.

**Plan to meet** as a group and bake the bread recipe in this essay using the prayers and thoughts provided in the text. Take time to enjoy one another as you bake and break bread together.

## 11. *The Hemorrhaging Woman* —————————

**Pray and meditate** on Mark 5:25–34.

**Follow** the steps in Lectio Divina or Praying with Scripture and Imagination.

**Reflect** on the essay "We Have but Touched Your Hem."

**Journal and/or share:**

- What has been my most severe hemorrhage?
- What in my life needs the hem of Jesus? How do I become more open to the gift of touch?
- When have I offered the hem to another? Who in my life needs my available hem?

**Listen** to God asking you to examine where others in your life have hemorrhages.

**Write** a prayer for another suffering soul.

## 12. Mary, the Mother of Christ _____

**Pray and meditate** on John 19:23–27.

**Follow** the steps in Lectio Divina or Praying with Scripture and Imagination.

**Reflect** on the essay "Blessed Mary of the Storm."

**Journal and/or share:**

- What is my relationship with Mary, the mother of Jesus?

- In what ways has this relationship or my perceptions of her changed over the years?

- In what ways, if any, was I affected by natural disasters or other tragedies, such as September 11, 2001?

- How do I see the tender touch of Mary being expressed amid tragedy and suffering in our world? In my own life?

**Listen** to God calling you to see Mary of Compassion and to spread her works in the world.

**Write** a prayer for a more compassionate heart.

## 13. The Woman Who Found the Lost Coin _____

**Pray and meditate** on Luke 15:8–10.

**Follow** the steps in Lectio Divina or Praying with Scripture and Imagination.

**Reflect** on the essay "Rejoice with Me!"

**Journal and/or share:**

- What are the areas in my life where I seem to struggle with grasping and demanding?

- What might God be asking me to trust him with?

- Has there been a symbol in my life that speaks to my spiritual journey? What does that symbol mean to me?

**Listen** for God seeking you.

**Write** a prayer of one who has been found.

## 14. The Samaritan Woman _____

**Pray and meditate** on John 4:4–30.

**Follow** the steps in Lectio Divina or Praying with Scripture and Imagination.

**Reflect** on the essay "I Will Give You a Drink" and the poem "Tina's Jug."

**Journal and/or share:**

- In what ways do relationships in my home nurture or disturb my spiritual walk?

- In what ways do I struggle with unworthiness or pride?

- In what ways do I seek to give a drink to others?

**Listen** to God calling you to give a drink to others.

**Write** a prayer asking God to give you the strength, courage, and true humility to serve others.

## 15. Ruth

**Pray and meditate** on Ruth 1:1–18.

**Follow** the steps in Lectio Divina or Praying with Scripture and Imagination.

**Reflect** on the essay "I Will Follow You."

**Journal and/or share:**

- What is/was my relationship with my mother like?

- How have I surprised myself by following after my mother?

- In what ways am I different from my mother?

- In what ways have prayer and meditation helped me to understand my mother and our relationship better?

**Listen** to God calling you to a new healing of old wounds.

**Write** a reflection on your mother or another parental figure who is important in your life.

## 16. Hannah

**Pray and meditate** on 1 Samuel 1:1–28.

**Follow** the steps in Lectio Divina or Praying with Scripture and Imagination.

**Reflect** on the essay "Help Me to Relinquish My Own Desires."

**Journal and/or share:**

- Where in my life is there barrenness?

- What one thing has been the most difficult for me to relinquish? Have I done so yet? If not, why not?

- What is my struggle with surrender? How does it feel when I am able to let go?

- Considering that obedience is to my own inner authority, what makes obedience so difficult for me?

**Listen** for God asking you to relinquish something to him.

**Write** a prayer giving that something to God.

## 17. *The Bent-Over Woman*

**Pray and mediate** on Luke 13:10–17.

**Follow** the steps in Lectio Divina or Praying with Scripture and Imagination.

**Reflect** on the essay "I Was Lifted Up."

**Journal and/or share:**

- What things about life bend me over and compromise my emotional, physical, and/or spiritual health?

- What period of my life yielded the most stress, and how did God help me through it?

- In what ways do I still need the healing touch of Jesus?

**Listen** for God's voice beckoning you to greater health of mind, body, and spirit.

**Write** a prayer seeking God's help in caring for yourself.

# List of Poems

# Acknowledgments

## from Robin

Thank you,

Easton, for your love and patience, your listening ear and feedback, and for the tensions you have held with me throughout this project. Sharing the journey with you has been the greatest fulfillment of my life.

Fr. Chester Arceneaux, my boss and pastor, for the flexibility you allow in my schedule so that I can write, go on mission, and truly attempt to live a balanced life. Thank you for your support of all of my ministries at Our Lady of Wisdom, which have enabled me to follow my bliss.

Sr. Nina Vincent, OLOS, and Toni Viale for your editing expertise and loving support of this project.

Sr. Gloria Murillo, my spiritual director, for your amazing questions that allow me to never forget that God always answers my prayers.

Vicki Schmidt, national director of the Theresians World Ministry, and all my sister Theresians, most especially my Open Heart community, for being my anam ċaras.

Frank and Genie Summers and Sarah Spiehler of Family Missions Company, for introducing me to mission and to experiences that have undoubtedly changed my life.

Lyn. We really do understand each other, don't we, my sister? We may not always agree on the tough issues, but love has ruled both of our hearts. What a journey we have made! Thank you.

## *from Lyn*

to Robin Hebert, my writing partner, who always hangs in there when the going gets tough. Robin, we owe ourselves at least one glass of champagne!

to Henrietta Schilling, our librarian at the Milton Branch Library, who is enthusiastic about my work, and always gets me just the volumes I need from the parish library. She does it with such grace and happiness. She is a real asset to our community.

to Dee, my husband, who supports me in so many tangible ways, always anticipating what I might need. His love language is giving, and I appreciate it more and more as the years go by.

to my directees who teach me so much more than I ever could teach them. Thank you for your beautiful spirits.

to Theresians International, and for those who have worked to keep the organization strong across the world. The charism of this group is amazing and has shaped my life in ways I never imagined.

to Paula D'Arcy, Joyce Rupp, Macrina Weiderkehr, and other amazing women spiritual writers who have influenced my work and my spirituality in deep ways. Thank you for daring to write and to live lives drenched in Spirit.

# About the Authors

**LYN HOLLEY DOUCET** is the co-author of *When Women Pray* with Robin Hebert. She is also the author of *Water from Stones: An Inner Journey,* which won a Catholic Press Award in 2002, *A Healing Walk with St. Ignatius: Finding God in Difficult Times,* and *Healing Troubled Hearts: Daily Spiritual Exercises.*

She grew up on a cotton farm in north Louisiana, with three siblings, where she developed a deep love of the natural world.

She has fond memories of growing up in a loving community in her Methodist church in Bastrop. Lyn was welcomed into the Catholic Church in 1972. She is from a family that includes Methodists, Episcopalians, Baptists, and those of no organized religion. Lyn is very comfortable with diversity.

Her undergraduate degree is in Speech and English from Louisiana State University. She has a master's degree in education from the University of Louisiana/Lafayette. After being in public school work for twenty years with special needs children, she is now a spiritual director, retreat master, and composer and is pursuing a master's degree in counseling.

She is active at various retreat houses and for the Diocese of Lafayette. Her talks combine storytelling, biblical text, humor, and her personal witness in a highly informative and enjoyable format. Lyn directs people in prayer and

Ignatian spirituality at her home in Maurice. She has also taught *Artist's Way* and creativity courses at the University of Louisiana's leisure learning center. She has recorded an original series of guided Gospel meditations with Louisiana composer/musician Walter Poussan Jr.

She lives with her husband near Maurice, Louisiana; he is a residential contractor. Their son Jacques lives in Baton Rouge, Louisiana. Lyn and Dee have three dogs and two pet pigs! She and her husband cherish their friends new and old and love to cook for anyone who comes by. Lyn enjoys being outdoors, lots and lots of reading, gardening, swimming, and walking.

**ROBIN HEBERT** grew up "a good little Catholic girl" in New Orleans, the youngest of three. The night her father died in a tragic airplane crash, her journey began. She was ten years old. She completed her Catholic education in New Orleans and attended the University of Southwestern Louisiana (now University of Louisiana–Lafayette), receiving a master's degree in education.

Robin is the co-author of *When Women Pray* with Lyn Doucet. She has also been involved in ministry as a pastoral counselor, spiritual director, retreat leader, and professional speaker for more than twenty years. She has journeyed with hundreds who share her same desire for awareness and contemplative prayer. She now serves as a campus minister at Our Lady of Wisdom Catholic Church and Student Center on the University of Louisiana–Lafayette campus, offering her skills in spiritual direction, teaching prayer, and leading communities of students and parishioners in a deeper walk with God.

Past national president of Theresians of the United States, a global ministry for women seeking a communal faith experience, Robin maintains involvement with Theresians through the mentorship of new communities and participation in her own "Open Heart" Community. And along with her husband, Easton, she co-leads annual mission trips for the Theresian World Ministry to a poor village in Mexico.

Robin lives in Lafayette, Louisiana, with her husband, Easton. She is a mother of four, stepmother of two, and grandmother of nine. Robin cherishes daily prayer time, walking, gardening, and reading. She is passionate about living a simple, balanced lifestyle.

# *Of Related Interest*

**Leslie Williams, Ph.D.**
**WHEN WOMEN BUILD THE KINGDOM**
*Who We Are, What We Do, and How We Relate*

These women's stories show how they minister differently from men — how they use their relationships, hearts, and spirituality to build community, how they bring compassion to justice, peace to difficult and violent situations, and authentic spiritual experience to all that they do and are.

In the eyes of Christ, all people are equal — but not all are the same! This is especially true for men and women. This charming book of stories from women shows how they "do" ministry differently from men — how they use their relationships, hearts, and spirituality to build community, how they bring compassion to justice, peace to difficult and violent situations, and authentic spiritual experience to all that they do and are. These stories give insight into a woman's mind, heart, and spirituality.

Topics include: The Bible from a Woman's Point of View + The Three Wise Women + Food, Food, Food + Where Women Go to Relax + When One or Two Are Gathered + Creation + Giving Birth

0-8245-2363-6, paperback

crossroad

## *Also by Lyn Doucet and Robin Hebert*

### WHEN WOMEN PRAY
*Our Personal Stories of Extraordinary Grace*

"We are two ordinary women who, through God's grace, have had extraordinary experiences of prayer. In this book we share several of these experiences. We have no final answers about God, for in prayer we have experienced God as a beautiful dance of mystery. And yet... we know that in the presence of this dance of love we have been transformed. And we now desire to invite you into this sacred dance of daily communion with God." Includes original prayers and helpful tips for praying.

0-8245-2279-6, paperback

Please support your local bookstore,
or call 1-800-707-0670 for Customer Service.

For a free catalog, write us at

THE CROSSROAD PUBLISHING COMPANY
16 Penn Plaza, 481 Eighth Avenue
New York, NY 10001

Visit our website at
*www.crossroadpublishing.com*
All prices subject to change.

crossroad